FROM THE WISE WOMEN
OF ISRAEL:
Folklore and Memoirs

FROM THE WISE WOMEN OF ISRAEL:

Folklore and Memoirs

Compiled by

Doris B. Gold and Lisa Stein

BIBLIO PRESS   NEW YORK

Dedicated to those Jewish women,
past or present,
whose wise words
did not appear in this book
and to
The next hundred years of Jewish women's works
(1893—The First Congress of Jewish Women)

First printing, 1993
© Biblio Press, NY

Library of Congress Catalog Card Number 93-071036

From The Wise Women of Israel: Folklore and Memoirs,
    Compiled by Doris B. Gold and Lisa Stein

  ISBN 0-930395-18-2

                    Printed in the United States of America

*The gamma shown above and on the back cover, is a Jewish female
symbol from antiquity. It was found on women's clothing fragments
when Yigael Yadin, the archeologist, excavated the Bar Kochba cave
site of 133 C.E., south of Qumran near the Dead Sea in Israel,
and has since been known as an authentic artifact.*

Cover illustration is part of a 4th cent. sarcophagus from Vigna Randan-
ini, Rome.

Acknowledgments

We acknowledge with thanks assistance to the publisher in the preparation of this book by:

Ita Aber, Bonny Fetterman, Beth Haber,
Marcia Miller, Prof. Sandy Rikoon, Peninnah Schram,
Bea Stadtler, and Renata Stein.

Acknowledgments to publishers who kindly extended permissions for reprinted excerpts are indicated on the pages where the works appear.

Doris B. Gold is an author, editor of Biblio Press, and former university teacher of English. She has published in books and Jewish periodicals, with features on women in both Jewish and mainstream news media. Her master's thesis at Washington University, St. Louis, was on American folklore. Her vita appears in *Who's Who of American Women* and in other references.

Lisa Stein is a graduate of Barnard College. She spent several years as an account executive in corporate training before leaving to pursue her love of writing. Her work has focused on Jewish topics and has been published in *The Jewish Review* and in Bnai Or publications. She lives in New Jersey with her husband Richard, and two sons, Sam and Jared.

FROM THE WISE WOMEN OF ISRAEL:
Folklore and Memoirs

Contents

❋

Preface

About a decade ago, when modern Jewish women first became aware of their invisibility in many spheres of knowledge, this offering of a taste of Jewish women's wisdom would have been termed "compensatory." In the 1990's, we two women view ourselves as making creative additions to the "canon" of Jewish women's affirmations.

A Christian thinker, in welcoming feminization in the 80's, noted that "women enjoy the wisdom that accrues to the alienated."* It is not our intention here to argue pro or con the common perception that women are more or less proficient in abstract reasoning, thus displaying fewer wise dictums; that they are more or less morally sensitive or religious "by nature"; that their association with children may or may not be a "historical advantage."** These and other conventional observations (including that women are more physical and less imaginative, etc.) seem irrelevant when one confronts their wise thinking, which is often received with an instinctive sense of rightness, akin to recognizing poetry.

Jewish thinkers, without reference to gender, have seen Jewish wisdom as a "practical skill trained on many aspects of reality."*** Ben Sira, an 8th century philosopher, saw "chochma"—wisdom—as "not accessible to many." Rabbinic

---

*"The Feminization of God and Ethics," by Daniel C. Maguire, in *Christianity and Crisis*, Mar. 15, 1982, p. 59–67
**Ibid.
***Nathan Ausubel, in *The Book of Jewish Knowledge*, Crown Publishers, 1964. See esp. p. 76, "Chochma".

writings in pre-modern times contain negative statements about women, often in the same breath with positive ones. (Many have noted that Proverbs:31 provides the recipe for the ideal woman, seen largely as wife.) The introduction here by Prof. Livia Bitton-Jackson provides a wider view of biblical women's wisdom.

Our original search was to find folklore only which was not formulaic and exemplified these criteria: stories which featured women as important and positive figures; those which might contain a woman's wise retort, an action that solved a problem or that demonstrated ingenuity; especially those that might show enlightened self-interest. We also sought those stories that might have universal applicability; that were told in simple but resonant language. In the end, however, we found it difficult to discover a wealth of such nuggets in the available tales, for women were so often absent or depicted as shrews, satans, harlots, tricksters, demons, or sorcerers. We learned that in Jewish folklore of Oriental origin, which includes those of Indian, Persian or Arabic countries, women are often represented in an unfavorable light. Concludes one such collector, "The anti-feminist bias is particularly prominent in both Jewish and world folklore."* Talmudic sources themselves retell legends of illustrious men unable to resist the sexual temptations of seducing women. We could find no female Solomon; while "sages" were always male rabbis. Thus we were compelled to turn to Jewish women's writings themselves in both biography and autobiography, where women's own stream of consciousness and action could reveal the qualities we sought.

While we have not avoided writings about women's "achievements"—for the paradox of wisdom is that it does not necessarily lead to success or notice—we were unable to find suitable excerpts from famed Jewish women's lives in the quantity we would have anticipated. Instead, we found

---

*Haim Schwarzbaum, *Jewish Folklore Between East and West,*; Ben Gurion University of the Negev Press, Beersheva, Israel.

those essential anecdotal samplings that could "fit" with folklore. Thus, we have joined two genres in our beginning search for feminist "wisdom literature."

Certain themes in the folklore we thought bear out our search. There, "Skotsl Kumt," a bit of folksay, shows the sisterhood of truth among women. As is common in folktale, riddle-solving dictates wise conclusions, and here, not only sons, but daughters are the victors. In "The Clever Carver," the prince falls in love with the daughter for her sagacity and not for her beauty, which is so often the case in this genre. (But note the traditional "wise and beautiful" in both the "Innkeeper's Clever Daughter" and The Fisherman's Daughter," portrayed in biblical women as cited in the Introduction to this book.) Ingenuity is not the least of women's traits in "The Clever Wife," "A Woman Who Saves From Death," and in "The Most Precious Thing in the World." Concerning the inclusion of some Sendebar tales—those known as *Mishle Sendebar*, were derived from popular tales of the 12th century, translated into Hebrew from other Eastern languages. These became known in the West as The Seven Sages of Rome, a romance intended to teach about the wiles of women (also evil in the heart of a young man). We thought to show that this seldom-presented material exists, and to turn the tables with harmless results and reveal women's sexual cleverness.*

It is worth noting that in the memoirs we selected there are two by men who cite women's deeds: Isaac Bashevis Singer and Samuel Chotzinoff. (There are doubtless others in this vein, but for our purposes we focused on women's writings) The Singer excerpt shows a woman's wise use of charity; the Chotzinoff one the courage to persist, and also the "wise speech" which we found to be frequent in both the folklore and the memoirs.

"Gluckel's Missing Jew," "Table Talk," "Let God Worry a

---

*For an interesting discussion of the Jewish folklore transmitted by men concerning women's "erotic voice", see *Eros and the Jews* by David Biale, Basic Books, 1992, p. 8–9.

Little Bit," and the excerpts from Rachel Calof's memoir, are all rich in their sense of self. Throughout, especially in selections by Hannah Trager, Emma Goldman, Ernestine Rose, Kim Chernin and Faye Moskowitz, women's ability to speak out for social justice is evident. As to the courage of intellect to trick the enemies of survival, the excerpts from Alicia, Golda Meir, and Liselotte Bendix Stern, are representative of a deep mine that is now available in Holocaust and crisis testimonies of many periods of Jewish life.

We are acutely aware that these nuggets of women's wisdom in folktale and memoir are but a whisper in the many voices to be found by other searchers to come. We are mindful that "It is not required that you complete a task, but neither are you exempt from beginning it."*

DORIS B. GOLD AND LISA STEIN

---

*Pirke Avot (Ethics of the Fathers)

Prophecy Equals Wisdom:
Women in the Biblical Tradition

Livia Bitton-Jackson

In searching for definition one finds in Biblical or post-Biblical literature neither an explicit formulation of the concept of prophecy nor a hint as to what makes a prophet. Among the personalities designated as prophets in Israel are seven women: Sarah, Miriam, Deborah, Hannah, Abigail, Huldah and Esther. Elsewhere in the Talmud is the assertion that all the matriarchs were prophets, which adds Rebeccah, Leah and Rachel to the list. One wonders: what element in their makeup singles out these biblical heroines for inclusion in the category of prophets? Would that common denominator reveal a clue about prophetic prerequisites?

At first glance the category seems haphazard. But upon examining each woman within the context of her historic role, the unexpected conclusion about the nature of prophecy as it relates primarily to women is this: prophecy in women is tantamount to qualities of understanding, discernment, insight, intuition, comprehension and compassion — the basic ingredients of wisdom.

Woman appears on the stage of human history in three gradually evolving stages. She is first an unknown entity taking shape around the rib, "tzela" in Hebrew, of Adam, and is "named woman, 'isha,' because from man, 'ish,' this one was taken" (Gen. 2:23). In formulating Woman, the entity Man, emerges. No longer is the first human merely Adam, an undefined creature from the "adama," the earth, just one step above inanimate nature.

Adin Steinsaltz translates the word "tzela," not as "rib" but "side," and explains the phenomenon of woman's creation as a separation of the two sides. Adam was initially created an androgynous creature, a composite of male and female elements. With the removal of the feminine "tzela," the male aspect materialized: man was created as a consequence of woman's creation.

"And God built the tzela which he took from the adam into woman" (Gen. 2:22). From the root of the word "vayiven," "and He built," the Rabbis extrapolate the connotation of "bina," understanding, and conclude that "bina" is a fundamental, built-in, so to speak, faculty of woman.

"Bina" is understanding the essence of things, the gift of discernment; also the gift of logical insight. One who deduces a thing from the essence of another thing, the Rabbis teach us, possesses the quality of "bina." From all this we may infer that the process of deriving a concept by analogy is not only the logical but also the intuitive process. And so the basic ingredients of woman: understanding, discernment, insight, intuition, add up to wisdom.

The second stage is woman's encounter with the snake. It is a complex portrayal. Woman here is simultaneously the effect and the cause of seduction; she is "seducee" and seducer. First she yields to power; then wields it. No sooner is she seduced by the snake to eat from the forbidden fruit of the Tree of Knowledge than she seduces her man to do so.

I have always wondered about woman's punishment for her act of seduction. After all, the divine communication about the pain of childbirth also brings good news: the woman is to bear children. Her new role adds another dimension to her reality, which warrants a new name. Woman becomes "Hava," Eve, the mother of all living things, and enters a third stage of her evolution.

In her act of giving birth, the archetypal woman/mother is the first human to exercise "bina," prophetic insight, into the mystery of creation and the mystery of the divine-human dialogue. With her exclamation, "I have acquired a man with God" (Gen. 4:1), she gives prophetic testimony to her mystery.

In Sarah's history one incident emerges as central to her designation as woman/ prophet: her confrontation with Hagar for primogeniture, the right of inheritance. Hagar's son Ishmael was Abraham's firstborn and as such, entitled to primacy. In the words of the Torah text, however, "And Sarah saw the son of Hagar the Egyptian whom she had borne to Abraham making sport" (Gen. 21:9), rabbinic interpretation identifies "making sport" with immorality; and Sarah's stance as prophetic insight. By taking steps to remove Ishmael from the sphere of influence in Abraham's household, Sarah is given credit for maintaining the primacy for the heir ethically suited for the task. God's admonition to Abraham: "Everything that Sarah tells you, listen to her (Gen. 21:12)," divinely validated Sarah's stance. And so, at this crucial juncture of history, the Rabbis maintain that through her insight it was Sarah's role to determine the future course of history.

A generation later, the confrontation between Sarah and Abraham over the primacy of succession was reenacted between Rebeccah and Isaac. Just as Sarah whose prophetic wisdom prompted her to recognize the proper heir to Abraham's legacy, Rebeccah was given the task of choosing the right successor to Isaac. The crisis in the Rebeccah-Isaac confrontation was perhaps more acute. In the former, the controversy pitted Sarah's son against the son of a foreign concubine; in the latter, Rebeccah was called upon to make a choice between her own two sons, and she had the prophetic insight (Gen. Rabba 67:9) to choose the younger over the elder preferred by her husband.

I would like to interject here an astounding rabbinic dictum according to which "It is to the credit of the righteous women that our forefathers were redeemed from

Egypt" (Sot. 11). Being fully aware that the Egyptian bondage and the Exodus, watershed events in the evolution of Israel as a people, assume central roles also in terms of Jewish ethics and halakhah, I am puzzled by the extravagance of the rabbinic avowal. What was the virtue of women to warrant such appreciation? And who were the women the Rabbis single out for such unqualified praise? The answers to this and a few other lavish rabbinic declarations about women to be cited later, paint a fascinating collective picture of women's manifest prophetic wisdom.

We are told that the Hebrew midwives Shifrah and Puah defied, at the risk of their lives, Pharaoh's decree, because "they feared God and did not do as the king of Egypt commanded them, and let the children live" (Ex. 1:17), and as a reward for their courage "God granted a bounty to the midwives, and the nation multiplied and grew very mighty" (Op. cit. 1:20). And we are told that the Hebrew women in general possessed "great vitality" to produce in the face of adversity a mighty nation" (Op. cit. 1:19). With their vitality of spirit, the Rabbis comment, the Hebrew women kept their appearance attractive and boosted the morale of their men. As a consequence, the level of Hebrew procreation was high.

The same spirit of prophetic wisdom motivated young Miriam to admonish her father, Amram, "Your edict is harsher than that of Pharaoh; Pharaoh's edict is only against males but your edict is against both males and females" (Sot. 12-13a). Amram who, in his despair over Pharaoh's edict to drown every newborn Hebrew boy in the river had divorced his wife Yokheved; now at Miriam's prompting resumed marital relations. And all the other Hebrew men followed Amram's example. Rabbinic commentary credits Amram with the good sense of acknowledging Miriam's prophetic role in the birth of Israel's redeemer: "When Moses was born, the house filled with light, and Amram exclaimed, 'my daughter, your prophecy came true!' " (BB 120a). (In vain did I search, however, for a rabbinic reference to the fact that Miriam's prophecy also assured the birth of Moses' peers, the male members of the "mighty nation" [Ex. 1:19] he was destined to redeem.)

When she led the women in song and dance to celebrate Israel's deliverance at the Red Sea, "Miriam the prophetess, the sister of Aaron, took a timbrel in her hand, and all the women went out after her with timbrels and with dances. And Miriam responded to them in song: "Sing to the Almighty for He is highly exalted, horse and its rider He cast into the sea" (Ex. 15:20). One wonders where Miriam and the other women obtained musical instruments to accompany their song and dance? Had they not departed from Egypt in great haste, without time even to bake their bread? The Rabbis provide an answer within the context of women's prophetic wisdom and faith: "The righteous women of that generation were confident that the Holy-One-Blessed-be-He would perform miracles for them, and they had brought their timbrels with them from Egypt ... " (Rashi, quoting Mekhilta). Here righteousness is added to the gamut of ingredients that make up prophetic wisdom. Righteousness characterized the wise women of Israel, who in the midst of general chaos during the Exodus remembered a seemingly minor, yet poetic, item: to take musical instruments for the anticipated celebration of the events to occur.

The appreciation of righteousness as basic to prophecy became axiomatic to Jewish thought. A fascinating phenomenon, the Jewish sibyl Sambathe, comes to mind in this context. In her epic poetry written in Greek during the first century in Alexandria, Egypt, Sambathe saw righteousness as pivotal to the concept of prophecy in Judaism. In her analogy between pagan and Jewish prophecy she describes her people as:

> " ... neither concerned for the sun's course,
> Nor the moon's, nor for the monstrosities on earth ...
> Nor for the soothsaying, nor sorcery, nor incantations! ...
> But they are concerned about righteousness and virtue."*

Sambathe's ancestress Deborah, is considered among the greatest of Israel's epic poets. Cabalistic literature ranks Deborah's Ode of Thanksgiving, together with Hannah's prayer, "on a spiritual level unequalled by any other hymn of praise composed to God by anyone, anywhere, any time" (Zohar, Lev. 19b). Just like Miriam and her contemporaries, Deborah predicted ultimate victory over Israel's arch foe through divine intervention: "Arise, this is the day God shall give Sisera into your hands ... " (Judges 4:14).

In combining prophetic spirituality with pragmatism, Deborah conformed to the established pattern. She was the only Judge of the epoch who actually judged, and the only military leader who waged a war of national liberation. All the other battles during the period of the Judges were battles with the short-range objective of driving an intruder out of a specific area. Deborah's campaign and eventual victory rid the country of an implacable enemy, once and for all, and marked the ultimate decline of the Canaanite kingdom.

Abigail's pragmatic wisdom found expression within a much less dramatic framework. After David swore revenge against Abigail's husband Nabal the Carmelite, who had foolishly refused to give provisions in return for protection, Abigail took the initiative to deliver the requested supplies. Although it is reported that Abigail was one of the four greatest beauties of all time and even a mention of her name inspired lust (Meg. 15a), David was primarily impressed with her wisdom, and accepted her gifts. During their meeting Abigail challenged David's acumen with a ritual question, and when the latter replied that he could not investigate the problem until the morning, Abigail hinted to him that the death sentence David had pronounced on her husband should also be postponed until the morning.

Esther, considered another one of the four most beautiful women in the world (Meg. 15a; Esther R. 6:9), is singled out in rabbinic literature for her keen insight into the psychology of faith. The Rabbis explain that Esther concealed her Jewish

*Sondra Henry and Emily Taitz, *Written Out Of History: Our Jewish Foremothers,* N.Y.: Biblio Press, 1990, p. 41.

identity because she did not want her fellow Jews to rely on "having a sister in the palace" and neglect to pray for God's mercy (Esther R. 8:6). Later, when Mordecai protested against her timing of the three fast days on the 13th, 14th, and 15th of Nissan, pointing out that the 15th was the first day of Pesah, Esther admonished: "Jewish elder! Without the Jewish people, why should there be Pesah?" Mordecai recognized her wisdom, cancelled the scheduled Pesah festivities and replaced them with the fast Esther had decreed (Esther R. 4:16).

"Thus shall you say to the house of Jacob ... " (Ex. 19:3). By equating "the house of Jacob" with women in this terse preamble to the divine revelation on Mount Sinai, the Rabbis open a lively debate which in a sense culminates in the assertion that "The Torah was transmitted to the women first." (Ex. R. 21:2).

I believe this provocative assertion to be a companion piece to the dictum which assigns credit to women for our forefathers' redemption from Egypt. Why such excessive claim? One rabbinic rejoinder targets women's built-in "bina" in reasoning that although men are better equipped to appreciate the finer points, the Torah as a whole was presented to the women first because women have a superior capacity for grasping basic concepts. In other words, feminine aptitude for comprehending the essence of an idea is essential in integrating Torah teaching into a lifestyle; the male faculty for analytical inquiry into hidden nuances of meaning is of secondary importance. Another Rabbinic authority simply observes that "women are eager to perform mitzvot" (Ex. R. 25). The women's zeal in the performance of mitzvot is ample qualification for this solemn privilege and responsibility. I feel, however, that the most significant justification offered for the women's primacy is their role in teaching children "the ways of the Torah." Because of their intuitive capacity, their superior grasp of the essence of the matter, the women were designated as the bridge to the future.

Recent scientific studies have disclosed that the corpus callosum, a thick bundle of nerves connecting the brain's right and left hemispheres, is often wider in the brains of women than in men. This may allow for greater interaction between the hemispheres, resulting in women's intuitive superiority. It is quite fascinating to speculate about a biological basis for rabbinic assertions about women's superior capacity of insight. But does it really make sense that physiological factors should account for the power of prophecy? For the faculty of faith? "Women have greater faith than men" (Sifri, Num. 133). And for the depth of discernment? "Women have greater power of discernment" (Nid. 45b). For righteousness? "The righteousness of women is superior to that of men ... " (Sifri) For pragmatic wisdom? "The women built that which the men destroyed. The women did not support the spies, instead they requested inheritance in the Land. Therefore they did not die in the desert as the men did." (Midrash Tanhuma, Num. 21)

Women's gift of wisdom comprises the power of prophecy. Prophetic power is a glimpse into the secret of the grand design of history, an insight which impelled an appropriate pragmatic reaction. Within the parameters of that reaction each wise woman became a prophet and the mover of events. Each was pitted against a man — Sarah against Abraham, Rebeccah against Isaac, Miriam against Amram,

Deborah against Barak, Hannah against Eli the High Priest, Abigail against David, Esther against Mordecai. In each circumstance, it was the woman's wisdom which determined the future course of Jewish history.

✳

Livia Bitton-Jackson is a professor of History and Jewish Studies at Lehman College, CUNY. She is the author of *Elli: Coming of Age in the Holocaust,* Times Books, 1980; for which she won a Christopher's prize in 1981. *Madonna or Courtesan? The Jewish Woman in Christian Literature,* Seabury Press, 1983; "Zionism in Hungary; The First Twenty-Five Years," *Herzl Year Book,* Herzl Press, 1971; "Judaism," *Americana Annual,* Grolier Inc., 1974-1989; "Israel," *Americana Annual,* 1976-1986, and others.

✳

Several parenthetical citations in this essay refer to Rabbinic literature as a source: Gen. Rabba (Genesis Rabba), Ex. R. (Exodus Rabba), Esther R. (Esther Rabba), Sifri, Mekhilta, Midrash Tanhuma — These are names of Midrashim. "Midrash" is a generic term denoting the extensive literature of legends, commentaries, homilies, ethical teachings and Biblical exegesis from the 4th to the 14th century. "Rabba" is a collective name of the Midrashim on the Pentateuch and the Five Scrolls. Sot. (Sotah), BB (Bava Batra), Meg. (Megiliah), Nid. (Niddah) — These are names of various tractates of the Mishnah and the Babylonian and Jerusalem Talmud.

FOR FURTHER READING

Berman, Saul. "The Status of Women in Halakhic Judaism." *Tradition* 14 (Winter): 5-28. 1973.

Bitton-Jackson, Livia. *Madonna or Courtesan? The Jewish Woman in Christian Literature.* New York: The Seabury Press, 1983.

Brayer, Menahem. *The Jewish Woman in Rabbinic Literature: A Psychohistorical Perspective.* Hoboken, N.J.: Ktav, 1986.

Ellinson, Eliakim, *The Woman and the Mitzvot.* Jerusalem: Alfa Press, 1979.

Ginzberg, Louis. *The Legend of the Jews,* (7 vols. 1909-38). Philadelphia: Jewish Publication Society.

Greenberg, Blu. *On Women and Judaism: A View From Tradition.* Philadelphia: The Jewish Publication Society of America, 1981.

Neusner, J. *A History of Mishnaic Law of Women.* Leiden: E.J. Brill, 1980.

Nunnally-Cox, Janice. *Fore-Mothers: Women of the Bible.* New York: The Seabury Press, 1981.

Reuther, Rosemary, ed. *Religion and Sexism.* N.Y.: Simon & Schuster, 1974.

Steinsaltz, Adin. *Nashim BaMikra.* Tel Aviv: Sifriyat "Universita Meshuderet," Dale Tzahal, 1984.

Swidler, Leonard. *Women in Judaism.* Metuchen, N.J.: The Scarecrow Press, 1976.

Trible, Phyllis. "Bringing Miriam Out of the Shadows," *Bible Review,* Vol. 5, No. 1, February 1989, p. 23.

PART I.
Folklore

The beginning of wisdom is to desire it.
SOLOMON IBN GABIROL

Lilith

Lilith, like Adam, had been created from the dust (adamah) of the earth and given to our first parent as his wife. But as soon as Lilith had joined Adam, the two began to quarrel, each refusing to be submissive and subservient to the other. "I am your lord and master," thundered Adam, "and it is your duty to obey me." But Lilith was not so easily tamed. Mockingly she retorted: "Are we not both equals? Have we not both issued from dust? I will not be submissive to you." Thus they quarreled and neither would give in. At last, weary of living with her spouse, Lilith uttered the Ineffable Name of the Creator and fled away, soaring up to regions celestial.

The above is abbreviated from the 7th century *Sepher Ben Sira*, ed. Steinschneider, 1858. See also *LILITH* Magazine, v. 1, #1, Fall, 1976 for essays on *LILITH* legends by Aviva Cantor. See other Lilith citations in the Bibliography.

✳

Skotsl Kumt: Skotsl's Here

You know that among Yiddish speakers, the expression *Skotsl kumt*, "Skotsl's here," is used by women to
greet another woman when she comes into the house.
Would you like to know its origin? I'll tell you a story
that will explain it.

Once upon a time the women complained that everything in the world belonged to men. Men got to perform
the *mitsves*, the religious commandments; they got
called to read from the Torah. In short, they got to do
everything. As for the women, they got nothing. No one
paid them any attention at all. So they decided to form
a deputation that would take their complaint to the
Lord of the Universe.

But how was it to be done? Well, they decided that
they would heap women up in a pile, one on top of the
other, until the woman at the very tip could pull herself
into heaven.

The first thing they did, then, was to dig a pit in which
one of the woman knelt. Then other women climbed on
her, one on top of the other. At the top of the pile was
Skotsl. Because she was both very clever and a skillful
speaker, she was chosen as the one to talk with the Lord
of the Universe.

From *Yiddish Folktales* by Beatrice Silverman-Weinrich, tr. by Leo-
nard Wolf. Copyright © 1988 by YIVO Institute for Jewish Research.
Reprinted by permission of Pantheon Books, a division of Random
House, Inc. NY.

Everything went well as the women were climbing onto each other. But just as Skotsl reached the top, the hunchbacked woman at the base of the pile twisted about, and the women came tumbling down. Well, of course there was nothing but noise and confusion, with everyone trying to locate everyone else. But Skotsl was nowhere to be found, though they searched for her everywhere. And so there was no one who could be counted on to talk with God, and the situation of the women remained unchanged. Everything still belonged to the men.

But from that time on, women have not lost their hope that one day Skotsl will come. And that's why, whenever a woman comes into a house, they call out joyfully, "*Skotsl kumt*, Here comes Skotsl," because who knows—one day she might really be there.

✳

About Beruriah

It was an ordinary Sabbath afternoon in the second century of the common era, but for Beruriah and her husband Meir, this Sabbath was marked for tragedy. Just before Meir returned from the house of study, Beruriah found their two young sons dead. Was it a sudden, unexpected plague, or the result of an illness? The sources are silent on the details of the death. What has remained of the story is Beruriah's wisdom and strength, her dignity in the face of this terrible loss.

Because it was the Sabbath, when mourning is not permitted, Beruriah did not tear her clothing, nor did she weep and wail. She placed the two boys on their bed and covered them with a sheet.

When Rabbi Meir entered, he asked for his sons. "Perhaps they are at the house of study," she answered evasively. Meir was surprised. He had just been there and had not seen them. Asking again for the whereabouts of his young sons, he sat down uneasily to his Sabbath meal. It was then that Beruriah put a question to him.

"Some time ago I was given two precious jewels to keep. But now the owner is claiming them from me unexpectedly. What shall I do?"

"Well, would you seriously think of keeping for your-

Rendered from Talmudic sources by Emily Taitz, co-author with Sondra Henry of *Written Out of History: Our Jewish Foremothers.* NY: Biblio Press, 1990.

self something that is the property of another? What was given in trust, must be returned," replied Meir.

Only then did Beruriah take her husband by the hand and lead him to the room where their dead sons lay. She uncovered them for him to see, whereupon the father began to weep.

"Do not cry," she said sorrowfully. "Did not you yourself say that what does not belong to us we must return? God has claimed our sons. May His name be a blessing."

* * *

Beruriah was known for her quips and her ironic answers to questions. One day, Rabbi Yossi the Galillean (*HaGlili*) was walking along the road. When he saw Beruriah, he asked: "What is the direction to Lod?"

"Imbecile from Galilee," she snapped back, "that [question] is too long. You should have said: 'Which way to Lod?'"

To impress him even further, she slyly reminded him: "You should know that the sages have commanded us not to talk too much with women."

* * *

One day Beruriah was walking along the road with her husband when they were annoyed by highwaymen. Meir complained of their constant presence in the neighborhood and expressed a wish for their deaths. Beruriah reprimanded him gently, saying: "Hate the sin and not the sinner. Pray instead for the sins to vanish."

Legend tells us that Meir took Beruriah's advice and the highwaymen repented.

* * *

Once, when Beruriah found a student learning his Talmud in an undertone, rebuking him for his lack of will, she said, "If you are not learning with your two hundred and forth-eight limbs and also with your organs of speech, your learning will not be sure!"

* * *

Beruriah (sp. Brurya, and various) lived in the second century CE and was the wife of the famed Rabbi Meir. She was one of the few women mentioned in the Talmud who had decisive opinions, and the only one whose statements were accepted as law. She was held in great respect by the other scholars of her time. In response to a student who proposed to learn a commentary on Chronicles in only three months, Rabbi Johanan first threw a clod [of earth] at him. Then he explained: "Even Beruriah, who was able to learn three hundred laws a day, from three hundred teachers, nevertheless took three years to truly master them. How, then, do you think you can do it in three months?"

✳

The Most Precious Thing
in the World

There was once a woman in Sidon who had been married to her husband for ten years but remained childless. He decided accordingly to be divorced, and went to consult Rabbi Simeon ben Yohai.

In vain did the Rabbi dissuade the man from divorcing his wife whom he professed to love, and at last he thus addressed him:

'You made a feast when you got married, and it is my advice that you should also separate after a banquet and part good friends.'

The couple followed the Rabbi's advice and caused a feast to be prepared at which the wife made her husband drink much wine.

"My dear," he said to his spouse whom he was about to leave, "take the most precious things out of my house with thee before leaving."

Now what did the woman do? When her husband was fast asleep she ordered her servants to carry him with his bed to the house of her father, and when the man awoke in the middle of the night and found himself in strange surroundings, he asked in some surprise: "Where am I?" To which his wife replied: "Thou art in the house of my father."

From *The Folklore of the Jews* by Angelo S. Rappoport, London: Soncino Press, 1937.

"And what have I to do in thy father's house? And how am I come thither?" asked the man in astonishment.

"I have acted upon thy own instructions," sweetly replied the young wife. "Last evening thou didst tell me to take away with me the most precious thing in the house, but there is nothing more precious to me in the world than thyself."

The husband was greatly moved and in the morning the couple went again to consult Rabbi Simeon ben Yohai, and the pious Rabbi prayed on their behalf to God and they had a son.

✻

The Clever Carver

A parallel to the Talmudical story of the clever carver is found in an Albanian tale which runs as follows:

One day a poor man received a prince as his guest and a cock was killed in his honour and placed on the table. The host's daughter was asked to carve the fowl and she did it in the following manner: She gave the head to her father, the body to her mother, and the wings to the prince, and took the flesh for herself and the younger children. Her father, though greatly astonished and even annoyed at the manner in which his daughter had carved the cock, was ashamed to rebuke her in the presence of the distinguished stranger. When they had retired from the night he could no longer restrain his impatience to know why the girl had cut up the fowl so badly.

"Why didst thou let our guest go to bed quite hungry?" he asked, to which the clever daughter replied:

"I will tell thee, father. I gave the head to thee, because thou art the head of this house, and I gave the body to mother, because she is like a ship which has borne us in her sides. The prince will take flight tomorrow and leave us, and therefore I gave him the wings. As for the children, they are the flesh of the

From *The Folklore of the Jews* by Angelo S. Rappoport, London: Soncino Press, 1937.

house, and therefore I gave them the flesh." Now the prince who had overheard her explanation marvelled greatly at her sagacity, fell in love with her and finally married her.

❦

A Woman of Valor Saves from Death

On the first anniversary of his marriage a husband went out to the forest, as was his wont, to cut wood, and his wife followed him. On that day the sun was dark in the heavens and no living thing was to be seen. Even the birds were silent. At noon, when the sun was at its height, the Angel of Death appeared with a large slaughterer's knife in his hand. He wielded the knife over the head of the husband who sank dead to the ground. When the woman saw that her husband was dead, she turned to the Angel and said: "Angel! I insist in the name of the one who sent you that you tell me why you have robbed me of my husband. Man's years upon this earth are seventy, and my husband is only twenty-one."

The Angel of Death replied: "Poor foolish woman! It is the decree of the Creator, and I cannot disobey it."

"If that is so," saith the woman, "Then I will ask you to fulfill my only wish."

"Whatever you ask me to do, I will do," said the Angel. "But I cannot restore your husband to life."

"I do not ask you to restore my husband to life," said the woman. "But I will ask you to restore the sight of the eyes of my father-in-law."

From *Moroccan Jewish Folktales* by Dov Noy. 1966. © Reprinted with permission of Herzl Press, NY.

"It shall be so," promised the Angel of Death.

Then she addressed the Angel of Death again: "Promise me, I beg you, that it shall be granted my father-in-law to see a grandson or great-grandson playing by his side.

"It shall be so!" the Angel of Death promised again.

Then said the woman: "I am the wife of the son of my father-in-law. I am the only one who is capable of giving birth to sons and daughters who will carry on his seed. If you indeed wish to honour your promise then you must restore my husband to life, for my husband had no children, and without his children my father-in-law will have no grandchildren or great-grandchildren. He who preserves one soul of Israel, has preserved a whole world. If you rob me of my husband, you rob me and my husband of my children, and my father-in-law of his grandchildren and great-grandchildren. You will break your promise and in one stroke you will destroy whole worlds."

The Angel of Death was at a loss as to what he should do. He had no choice but to restore the woman's husband to life. And the moment the Angel of Death rose into the heavens the woman's husband stood once again on his feet.

The woman and her husband returned to their hut and found the old man reciting the benediction: "Blessed be he who opens the eyes of the blind." They all rejoiced at the miracles that had been wrought for them and recited the blessing: "Blessed be who restores souls to dead bodies."

Common sense is the root of wisdom.
SAMUEL HANAGID

There is no bad mother and no good death.
YIDDISH SAYING

✿

The Fisherman's Daughter

Once there was a fisherman whose wife had died and left him with their young child. This child, named Esther, grew to be a beautiful young woman, and she loved her father very much. She helped him in every way she could, especially by doing what needed to be done in the house. Every day, the fisherman went down to the sea to fish. Then he would sell his catch in the marketplace and use the money to buy any provisions needed for himself and his daughter.

Near their house lived a poor widow who often chatted with Esther. One day, the widow said, "You should urge your father to marry so you would have a mother to help take care of the house. A young girl should not have to work so hard without someone to help her. Why not suggest to your father that he marry *me*. I will be a good mother to you and do all the housework. You will be like a true daughter to me."

That evening, Esther said to her father, "Dear Father, I do all the housework with a glad heart. But sometimes it becomes so difficult and lonely for me to work alone all day while you are fishing." And the daughter suggested that perhaps her father would consider the neighbor-woman. "After all, she is alone too, Father, and

From *Jewish Stories One Generation Tells Another* by Peninnah Schram. Reprinted with permission of the publisher, Jason Aronson, Inc., Northvale, NJ © 1987.

together we could become a family. I know she will be good to us and take care of me and help me."

The fisherman had been reluctant to marry for fear that a new wife would deal harshly with his daughter. But Esther pleaded with her father until finally he agreed to marry the widow.

In the beginning the widow acted kindly to the daughter, but slowly, slowly, she became more demanding and soon left all the housework for Esther to do.

When the father saw how his daughter grew sadder and sadder, he realized what was wrong. So one day he said, "Esther my child, come with me to the seashore. I am not as strong as I was before, and I need your help in my work." From then on, Esther went with her father every day. The two enjoyed being together, and Esther was even able to help her father sometimes. And so it went, day after day.

One day, the fisherman cast his net but could not pull it in, for it was too heavy. Even though Esther helped, they could not succeed in pulling it in. So the father said, "Hold the ropes, my daughter, and I will run for some strong men to help me."

As Esther was holding the ropes, she heard a melodious voice calling from the depths of the sea, *"Let me go and I will do you much good. I will also fill the net with the best fish."*

Esther was surprised to hear the voice and listened to the strange request, but she held the ropes tighter than before, as her father had instructed her to do. After more pleading, Esther released some of the net's ropes.

Suddenly, a beautiful mermaid-princess arose from the sea, and she said to Esther, *"Take some of my hair. Because of this favor to me, I will reward you. If you ever need my help, burn a single hair and I will come to you immediately and do as you ask."*

Then the mermaid-princess disappeared, and in her

hand Esther held some of the mermaid's long strands of hair.

When Esther's father returned moments later with several men, they managed to pull in the heavy net and saw that it was filled with the best fish, which they sold at a great profit.

Esther's stepmother hated her for going off with her father every day and not helping her at all. And she grew more and more jealous every time she heard the fisherman talking and laughing with Esther as they left to go to the seashore each morning or on their return home each evening.

Time passed, and the stepmother vowed to herself to find a way to be rid of her stepdaughter.

In that kingdom lived a Queen who loved to walk along the seashore collecting shells and listening to the sound of the waves breaking against the shore. One day, at a time when the Queen was expecting a child, she was enjoying the sea air. A magician suddenly appeared and swore his love for the queen. The Queen rejected his advances and shouted, "You act like a snake, not a gentleman."

The magician, hearing this, replied, "Oh, my Queen, a snake?" And he disappeared as quickly as he had appeared, but not before turning the child in the Queen's womb into a snake. (The Queen, of course, did not know what was happening. How could she know?)

When it was time for the Queen to give birth, they brought the midwife to the palace. As she was attending the queen, the midwife suddenly fell ill and died. Each midwife that came close to the Queen died. The King declared, "Whoever can successfully attend the queen in this birth will be richly rewarded."

Esther's stepmother, hearing the King's proclamation, thought to herself, "I will send the fisherman's daughter to the queen. This will put an end to her life, and I will be rid of her."

So the stepmother sent a message to the palace that Esther, the fisherman's daughter, was an expert midwife. The King's messenger brought Esther to the palace. When she arrived, Esther changed her clothes and, remembering the mermaid's offer of help, burned one of those long hairs she kept with her.

Immediately, the mermaid-princess appeared and said, "*Do not be afraid, but follow all that I say. Ask the King for a large pot filled with honey. Put the pot on the fire and, while it is heating, bring the Queen into the room and close the door. When the pot of honey boils, the smell will entice the infant to come out of the womb. Know that the infant will be in the skin of a snake, but do not be afraid of it. And, above all, refuse any gift from the King.*"

Esther did all that she was instructed to do. The queen gave birth to a child in the skin of a snake, and she began to nurse it. Esther refused to accept any payment from the King and returned home.

The child grew, and when he was five, the King hired a tutor to instruct him in Torah and royal manners. But as soon as the tutor came near the child, he immediately fell dead. The same fate befell each of his tutors. So the King proclaimed throughout the kingdom, "Whoever can teach my child Torah and wisdom will be greatly rewarded."

Again the stepmother sent a message to the palace: "The fisherman's daughter," she said, "is an excellent teacher." Esther was brought to the palace, where she changed her clothes and burnt another of the mermaid's hairs.

The mermaid-princess appeared and said, "*Fear not. Ask the King for two rooms adjoining one another. Place rare and delicious fruit in the first room. In the second room place the Torah and books in the seventy tongues of the world. When the prince enters the first room, feed him some of the sweet fruit. Then bring him to the room with the books. Whatever book you give him, he will learn easily. Soon he will know all the languages, and he will be wise in the ways of Torah. But remember, do not accept any gift from the King."*

Esther did as the mermaid told her to do, and the prince learned well. Although the King offered her great rewards, she refused to accept anything and returned home.

The child grew and became a wise and kind young prince. When he turned eighteen, his parents began to seek a wife for him among the nobility. But every girl who came near him immediately fell dead. The King and Queen were upset by their son's fate and they proclaimed, " A great prize will be given to the woman who succeeds in forming a union with our son."

Esther's stepmother hastened to inform the palace, "The fisherman's daughter would like to wed the prince."

The King's emissary brought Esther to the palace. As before, she changed her clothes and burnt one of the mermaid's hairs. The mermaid-princess immediately appeared before her and spoke.

"Do not be afraid, for although the task before you is difficult, you will succeed if you do as I say.

"Ask the King for three adjoining rooms which will be closed to everyone but you and the prince.

"In the first room, light a wood fire in the fireplace.

"In the second, prepare a bathtub full of lukewarm water.

"And in the third, place a bed with a mattress of ostrich feathers.

"Put on seven more dresses, one on top of the other, and go with the prince to the heated room. Remember, and this is important, instruct the King and Queen that no one is

——— 17 ———

to come into the room, even if they hear the prince scream-
ing. And you, too, must not pay any attention to the
screaming.

"Then command the prince, saying, 'When I take off
one of my dresses, you must take off one of your skins.'
After his screams fade, he will shed his first skin. Then
immediately take off a second dress and command the
prince to cast off a second skin. Each time he will scream,
but he will shed one of his seven skins. Finally, only your
own dress will remain. Take the seven dresses and seven
skins and burn them in the wood fire.

"Then go into the second room and command the prince
to bathe in the tub of warm water. Scrub him and wrap
him in a large robe. Then take the prince into the third
room and command him to lie in the bed. And you lie
down, too, but remain fully clothed and keep a pillow be-
tween you. All will be well if you do all that I have told
you."

Esther followed the mermaid's instructions, and the
prince shed all his seven snake skins, while screaming
terribly. No one dared enter the room, and everything
happened as the mermaid had predicted.

The next morning, the King opened the door and
found his son and the young woman lying in the bed.
Instead of the snake, he saw a handsome young man
whose face shone with beauty. And the young woman,
who the King feared was dead, was not dead at all, but
more alive and more beautiful than ever.

The two young people were dressed in royal garments
and brought before the King and Queen. The King and
Queen embraced their son and, with hearts full of gratitude, they warmly thanked the fisherman's daughter for
all the help she had given their son through the years.

During this time, the prince had fallen in love with
the wise and beautiful Esther. He spoke to her with

words of love and asked his parents for consent to marry her.

"No," replied Esther, "I thank you for this great honor, but I am a fisherman's daughter. I am not fit to be the wife of a prince."

"If, as you say, you are not fit to be the prince's wife only because you are a fisherman's daughter," said the prince, "then I now appoint your father to be my vizier. You are no longer a fisherman's daughter, but the daughter of a vizier."

Since the King and Queen were very fond of this wise young woman, they gave their consent.

And Esther, who loved the prince, then gave her approval, too.

When the fisherman's wife, whose jealousy of her stepdaughter had been so great and whose schemes to get rid of Esther had all failed, heard all this, she ran into the sea and drowned.

Esther, the vizier's daughter, and the prince were married in a majestic wedding, and they lived long and happy lives filled with love and wisdom and joy.

✳

An Offspring's Answer

There once was a mother bird who knew it was time to migrate to warmer lands. In order to get to the place where she went every year, she would have to cross a great sea. She began to get ready for the long journey. Knowing that her three fledglings were too young yet to fly, especially over such a great distance, she decided to take the three little birds on her back. She loved her children, and she was willing to do anything in the world for them.

And so the little birds got on their mother's back, and the mother bird began to fly. At first, the flight was easy enough. "Carrying my own young is never too burdensome," thought the mother bird. But as time went by, the little birds began to feel heavier and, after the first day, then the second and finally the third day, the mother bird was tired.

"My child, my birdling," asked the mother bird of the little bird sitting in front, "Tell me the truth. When I get old and will have no strength to fly across such an ocean, will you take me on your back and fly me across?"

"No mama," answered the fledgling.

"What? You disregard the *mitzva* of respect for your

From *Jewish Stories One Generation Tells Another* by Peninnah Schram. Reprinted with permission of the publisher, Jason Aronson, Inc., Northvale, NJ © 1987.

parent?" said the mother bird. And in anger she threw the little bird into the sea.

Then she turned to the second of her young and said, "Tell me the truth, my child, my birdling. When I get old and will have no strength to fly such a great distance, will you take me on your back and fly me across?"

"No mama," answered the second fledgling.

Again the mother bird became angry. "Indeed! You disregard the *mitzva* of respect for your parent." And the mother bird threw the young one into the sea.

With a hurt-filled heart, the mother bird turned to the third fledgling. Speaking in a guarded tone, she asked, "My child, my dear sweet fledgling, tell me the truth. When I get old and will have no strength to fly over such a big sea, will you take me on your back and fly me across?"

And the third fledgling answered, "My mother, I can't promise to do that. I may not be able to fly you across a sea because I may be busy flying my own children on *my* back just as *you* are doing for *me*."

When the mother bird heard this answer, she laughed with a joyful sound, and she and her fledgling continued on their flight.

Every woman has a mind of her own.
TALMUD

Little girl, don't be so sweet—lest you be consumed.
YEMENITE PROVERB

The Innkeeper's Clever Daughter

Once there was a nobleman and he had three Jewish tenants on his estate. One held the forest concession, another operated the mill, the third, the poorest of them, ran the inn.

One day the nobleman summoned the three and said to them, "I am going to put to you three questions: 'Which is the swiftest thing in the world? Which is the fattest? Which is the dearest?' The one who answers correctly all of these questions won't have to pay me any rent for ten years. And whoever fails to give me the correct answer, I'll send packing from my estate."

The Jew who had the forest concession and the one who operated the mill did not think very long and decided between them to give the following answers: "The swiftest thing in the world is the nobleman's horse, the fattest is the nobleman's pig, and the dearest is the nobleman's wife."

The poor innkeeper, however, went home feeling very much worried. He had only three days' time to answer the nobleman's questions. He racked his brains. What answers could he give?

Now the innkeeper had a daughter. She was pretty and clever.

From *A Treasury of Jewish Folklore* edited by Nathan Ausubel. Copyright © 1948, 1976 by Crown Publishers, Inc. Reprinted with permission of Crown Publishers, Inc.

"What is worrying you so, father?" she asked.

He told her about the nobleman's three questions.

"Why shouldn't I worry?" he cried. "I've thought and thought but I cannot find the answers!"

"There is nothing to worry about, father," she told him. "The questions are very easy: The swiftest thing in the world is thought, the fattest is the earth, the dearest is sleep."

When the three days were up the three Jewish tenants went to see the landowner. Pridefully the first two gave the answers they had agreed upon beforehand, thinking that the landowner would feel flattered by them.

"You're wrong!" cried the nobleman. "Now pack up and leave my estate right away and don't you dare to come back!"

But, when he heard the innkeeper's answers he was filled with wonder.

"I like your answers very much," he told him, "but I know you didn't think them up by yourself. Confess— who gave you the answers?"

"It was my daughter," the innkeeper answered.

"Your daughter!" exclaimed the nobleman in surprise. "Since she is so clever I'd very much like to see her. Bring her to me in three days' time. But listen carefully: she must come here neither walking nor riding, neither dressed nor naked. She must also bring me a gift that is not a gift."

The innkeeper returned home even more worried than the first time.

"What now, father?" his daughter asked him. "What's worrying you?"

He then told her of the nobleman's request to see her and of his instructions.

"Well, what is there to worry about?" she said. "Go to the market-place and buy me a fishing net, also a goat, a couple of pigeons and several pounds of meat."

He did as she told him and brought to her his purchases.

At the appointed time she undressed and wound herself in the fishing net, so she was neither dressed nor naked. She then mounted the goat, her feet dragging on the ground, so that she was neither riding nor walking. Then she took the two pigeons in one hand and the meat in the other. In this way she arrived at the nobleman's house.

The nobleman stood at the window watching her arrival. As soon as he saw her he turned his dogs on her, and, as they tried to attack her, she threw them the meat. So they pounced on the meat and let her pass into the house.

"I've brought you a gift that is not a gift," she said to the nobleman, stretching out her hand holding the two pigeons. But suddenly she released the birds and they flew out of the window.

The nobleman was enchanted with her.

"What a very clever girl you are!" he cried. "I want to marry you, but only on one condition, never must you interfere with my affairs!"

She gave him her promise and he made her his wife.

✿

King Solomon and Queen Keshira

Once upon a time, King Solomon sought to marry a beautiful queen whose name was Keshira. The queen agreed on one condition: that first he build her a palace made entirely of eagle bones.

So Solomon decreed that all the eagles in the world should take their own lives, so that there would be enough bones to build the queen's palace. The eagles went to the owl and told him of their plight. "I'll go to Solomon," said the owl, "and tell him what harm a woman can bring to the world. In fact, I'll convince him what a mistake it is to value women at all."

And that is what the owl attempted to do. It went to the king and told him the following story.

"There was once a woman," said the owl, "who loved her husband dearly. The two of them lived happily together and swore to be true to each other even in death. One day the husband died and was buried, and the wife went to the graveyard to mourn him. That same day, it so happened, a blind man stole money from the royal treasury and was caught, and the king handed him over to the grand vizier to be executed. On the way to the gallows, however, the blind thief escaped, and try as they might, the policeman could not find him. The one place they forgot to look was in the graveyard, and so the grand vizier went there himself, hoping to find the thief. When he saw the woman mourning at her husband's grave, he told her what had happened. "Why let it worry you, sir?" said the woman. "Here lies my newly buried husband who was blind himself toward the end of his life—you need only dig him up and cast his body at the feet of the king in place of the thief who escaped. Who will know the difference?"

And the owl concluded, "From this, Your Majesty, you can see what a woman's word is worth."

Then King Solomon said to the owl, "I too have a story to tell."

"Once," the king related, "there was a loving couple who lived happily and lacked for nothing. One day the husband came into possession of some fine merchandise, and though he could have sold it for a large profit in the capital, he did not go there, being loath to leave his wife alone. Yet the woman, sensing that her husband was unhappy, asked him for the reason, and when told it, urged him to make the trip at once. And so he listened to her and set out—only to be arrested by the king upon reaching the capital and thrown into prison. The woman waited and waited for him, and when at last she found out what had happened, she put on her best clothes and went to the king's court to ask for her husband back. The king and his grand vizier replied that they would grant her wish on the condition that she lie with them both. And so it was agreed that they would come to her lodgings the next day.

"The woman returned to her lodgings, removed the rugs from the floor, and smeared glue all over it. When the king and his grand vizier came the next day, they slipped as they entered the room and stuck to the floor. The woman locked the door and told them, "If you want to be freed, you yourselves had better free all your prisoners." The king begged in vain to be allowed to free only the woman's husband, but in the end he had to promise her what she asked for and put it in writing, stamped with the royal seal. The next day, she went and stood by the prison gates in order to see the prisoners freed. A huge throng of them, some thirty thousand men, was liberated from bondage, and among the last to emerge was her husband. And so you see, O owl, what a woman's word and devotion are worth."

Thus King Solomon concluded his story, after which he took Queen Keshira for his wife.

Vashti

R. Abbahu said: "When Israel eats and drinks they engage in words of Tora and songs before the Holy One. But when the nations of the world eat and drink they engage in indecent talk." These said, "The Median women are the most beautiful," and the others said, "The Persian women are the most beautiful." Ahasuerus said to them: "The vessel* I am using is not from Media and not from Persia, but from Chaldea, and there is none like it in the whole world!" He said to them: "Do you wish to see her?" They said to him: "We do, provided that she be naked."

Thereupon Ahasuerus commanded that they bring Vashti the queen before the king with the royal crown (Esth. 1:11), that nothing should be on her except the crown, and that she be naked.

But the queen Vashti refused (Esth. 1:12). She sent him words which touch the heart. She said to him: "Why do you demand this? If they find me ugly, you will be disgraced, and if they find me beautiful, they will plan to kill you and will violate me."

When the king insisted she sent him this message: "O, you fool, your heart went out because of your wine. Know that I am the daughter of Belshazzar, the son

*Possibly also "vassal"; a subject or a dependent.

From *Gates To The Old City* by Raphael Patai © Detroit: Wayne State University Press, 1981. Reprinted with the permission of the author.

of Nebuchadnezzar who was praised among kings, and rulers were like nothing before him, and you could not have been even a chief of equerries in the house of my father, not even a questor to run before his chariot. Not even the convicts of my father were judged naked."

And the king was very wroth and his anger burned in him (ibid.). R. Yoḥanan said: "All those seven years from the time when Vashti was executed until the time when Haman was crucified, his anger burned in him."

When Ahasuerus sobered up from his wine he asked for Vashti. They said to him: "You had her killed." He said to them: "Why?" They said to him: "Because you said she should come before you naked and she did not come." He said to them: "I did wrong. Who gave me the advice to kill her?" They said to him: "The seven princes of Persia and Media." He had them killed instantly.

It is a duty to save a woman from rape,
even at the cost of the assailant's life.
SIMEON BAR YOCHAI

Job's Novella

I heard the cry of a maiden from the land of Egypt, a young woman of good family, an innocent virgin. She was captured beyond the Nile River by pirates, who brought her to the land of Ethiopia. There they sold her to a wealthy nobleman, one of the brothers of Nabal the Carmelite, who was like him in being a Calebite. As soon as this man glimpsed the girl's good taste, her beauty, and fine intelligence, he purchased her in order to maltreat her and take her virginity. At first he spoke to her in a pleasant and comforting way, "Don't be afraid. You will be like a daughter to me." The girl prostrated herself before the man and worked for him as a maidservant with such great diligence that she was equal if not superior to anyone who made light of her.

The man fell in love with the woman. One day he found her alone in the house and revealed his deepest feelings to her. He promised her that if she submitted to him, he would give her a dowry, free her, and marry her to one of his servants. The girl refused. She wept and begged him not to do so shameful a thing as to take her virginity. Besides, this would make her a rival to his wife, who is like his own flesh; she would only be jealous of another [woman]. The young girl acted

From *Rabbinic Fantasies,* Imaginative Narratives from Classical Hebrew, Eds. D. Stern and M.J. Mirsky. © 1990. Reprinted with permission of the Jewish Publication Society of America, Philadelphia.

wisely. She left the wicked man, and he did not carry out his intentions. Every day, however, he continued to implore her. Yet she did not submit, even to his request to sleep with him without having intercourse. Instead, she grew more modest. But when she saw that he continued every day to try her, she finally said to herself: Eventually I will be unable to escape from him. He is my master, and his desire is intense. Vast floods will not quench love. He will chain me by my legs. Who knows if I will be able to escape from the snare and from the pit? Now is the time to seek advice in order to flee from under his net lest that slothful man hunt his prey.

Accordingly, the girl went to her mistress, and, weeping bitterly, she revealed to her in secret exactly what had happened. When her mistress saw that the girl was about to cry, she recognized the truth, for truth follows its own course. And she told her, "Be quiet. Do as I command you." The girl answered: "I will do whatever you command. I am your maidservant, and I place my soul and my virginity in your hands. I hope you will rescue me."

Her mistress gave her the following instructions: "Listen, my daughter. Observe your master when he speaks and tempts you again, as is his regular custom. Tell him that you wish to fulfill his desire and will sleep with him that very night, at the middle of the second watch (1:30 A.M.), at a time when no one can be heard and the streets are deserted. But you will hide yourself somewhere and remain there. Meanwhile, I shall go in your place and keep your promise." The maiden bowed and prostrated herself, and did just as her mistress had commanded her.

Only a short time passed before she spoke with her master. When the man heard that the girl would respond to his request at midnight, he was astonished and silently anticipated the appointed day and time.

So overjoyed that he was about to fulfill his desire, he stopped thinking about his wealth or property. That midnight, the man rose in the dark, closed the door behind him, and went to take his fill of love at the appointed place and to delight in lovemaking until the morning. When he arrived, he was so overwhelmed by passion that he trusted the woman's words, and because the place was dark, he did not recognize his wife. He drank from his cup while thinking it was another.

In the early morning, the man wished to depart before someone might recognize him and accuse him of having intercourse with the woman the previous night. But his wife asked him: "Where are you going so early in the morning? Where do you think you were sleeping all night? I am your wife, the woman of your youth, but you thought badly of me and turned your heart to arrogance, to Egypt, to the people that has ceased to be. Did you consider this to be just, a way to acquire for yourself a name and glory in your old age, now that you have lost your virility and youth? If ever this becomes public knowledge, how will you bear your shame and disgrace before all the old men with whom you take counsel?"

"But do this, and the affair will be known only between us. No one outside shall hear our voices. First, speak no longer with the maidservant, neither for good nor for bad, for this does not do you honor. What has happened is done; for the sake of our previous love, I shall be quiet and restrain myself. I shall be to you as before, obedient to your words and attentive to your voice. For you are my master; I shall bow down to you. But if you will not follow these instructions, and if you, the king, do not desire my beauty, and you turn your heart to this maidservant in our house, God will permit me to reveal your shame publicly, for my own sake. You will be disgraced. No longer will I be your wife. I will leave your house and go to my father's and brother's.

And this evil will be greater than anything you have experienced since the time of your youth."

When the man heard his wife's words, he turned to stone, stunned like a man seized by delirium. He had no idea whether he sat among the dead in this world or in the next. He feared for life and honor, and he was terrified by the words of his wife, a courageous woman, a daughter of nobility and stature, and a scion of an important family. So he changed his mind, spoke kindly to her and laughed. "Who would ever have thought," he said, "that an important person like me would be caught in a game of whores like some worthless person? What should I do? Passion corrupts the rules of conduct, and there is no protection against unchastity. Do not fear! I will not continue to act as I have. My fantasy was satisfied by spending the night with you; my obsession is there. The passion that was in my heart has receded, but my soul cleaves still to you."

The woman graciously accepted his words. The two arose, and no one besides her and her husband knew of the matter. From that day on, he no longer spoke to the maidservant.

*Give your ear to all, your hand to friends
but your lips only to your wife.*
YIDDISH SAYING.

When wisdom enters, subtlety comes along.
TALMUD

✳

The Clever Wife

Once there was a king who declared that he would only marry a woman who was willing to break off all relations with her parents after the wedding and never see them again. Despite this harsh condition, many women wished to be queen, and so the king held a contest to choose one of them to sit beside him on the throne. After the wedding, the king spent most days away from the palace attending to matters of state, and so his new wife was almost always alone. After several months she died of loneliness.

The king mourned her, and then declared another contest to choose a new queen. But this queen, too, he neglected, and she too died of loneliness. So it went for many years, queen succeding queen, and the king burying them all.

Once an only daughter wished to become the new queen. Her parents tried to discourage her, but she insisted on trying her luck in the king's contest.

"Do not worry, my dear Mother and Father," she told her parents before she left them. "I promise that I will see you again."

Since she was both beautiful and graceful, the king chose her for his new bride. After the wedding, he left her alone as he had all the others.

From *The Classic Tales: 4000 Years of Jewish Lore* by Ellen Frankel. Reprinted by permission of the publisher, Jason Aronson, Inc., Northvale, N.J. © 1989.

In a few days the new queen became bored. So she took a goatskin, blew it up, dressed it in men's clothing, and painted a face on it. Then she proceeded to pour out her sorrows to it.

Whenever the king was with her, she responded happily to his attentions, but when he was gone, she held long conversations with her doll. After several months, the king was surprised to find her so well and happy. None of his previous queens had adjusted so well to their solitary lives in the palace.

"Perhaps she is betraying me," he thought to himself.

So he drilled a hole in the wall of her bedroom and spied on her. And soon he saw her conversing with a strange man.

"Aha!" he said to himself. "So I am being deceived!"

Then he ordered his guards to watch if anyone was stealing in and out of her room. They watched carefully but discovered no one coming in or going out.

A few nights later, he concealed a dagger in his robe and invited his wife to come into his room. When she stood before him, he drew forth the dagger and demanded, "Where is your lover?"

"Come with me and I will show you," she said.

She led him to a cupboard in her room. The king flung open the door and plunged his dagger deep into the goatskin doll. Blood flowed from the doll onto the floor.

"What is this?" he cried.

She said to him, "This is my sorrow and my grief. If I had not told this doll all that was in my heart, I would have burst from all my suffering."

And at last the king understood that he had been the cause of his wives' deaths, and he repented of his hard heartedness. He revoked his cruel decree and invited his wife's parents to come visit her in the palace.

And so she kept her promise that she would see them once again.

✳

Some Tales of Sendebar

There once was a man who was ruled by a demon and, whenever he seized the demon, it responded to him.

And whenever someone lost something, or had a lover in another land, and the demon was asked, it would furnish the information. Now the demon had been with the man for two years, and the man had earned his living thereby.

And it came to pass, at the end of this time, that the demon said to the man:

"Know that my master sends me to the wars, and I won"t return. Come now, and I"ll teach you three incantations with which you can make three wishes of God and He"ll grant them to you."

So the man told his wife and he said to her: "Thus-and-thus did the demon instruct me. What do you advise me to ask of God?"

She said: "Try one incantation and if it works, we"ll know what to ask."

Then he said: "What should I wish for?" And she replied: "Ask God to cover your whole body with penises."

And he made the request, and it was fulfilled.

So he said to his wife: "What have you done?" And she replied: "Ask God to remove all the penises from you."

From *The Tales of Sendebar*, ed. Morris Epstein, Philadelphia, Pa.: Jewish Publication Society of America. 1967. Reprinted with permission of the publisher.

And they disappeared, including his very own, and he was left a eunuch. And he said:

"Now what have you done? I haven't even got one left!"

So she replied: "Well, you've got one incantation left. Request that your own be returned to you."

And he did and it was returned to him. Now he said: "What kind of advice did you give me? You did not counsel me to wish for wealth or wisdom."

So she said to him: "If you had suddenly grown rich, you'd have deserted me for another woman!"

There once was a pious man and he had a beautiful wife. Now when he used to go on business she'd bring her lover and lie with him.

Once it happened that the merchant returned from a far-off land. He came into the room and found the wall covered with phlegm. So he said to his wife:

"Don't say a thing. I know for certain that a man was here and that he slept with you."

She answered: "My lord, don't say that! For, from the day that you went out of your house, no man has touched me even with his little finger."

Now the husband did not believe her. So she said to him, "I'll take an oath on it."

So both of them went to take the oath. She sent to her lover saying that he should come to meet her—"and have in your hand an earthenware pot, and spill its contents when you see us and smash the pot."

That's what he did. And it happened when she stepped over it in the mud her foot slipped and she fell.

Whereupon her lover rose, took her in his arms, and said to her: "Arise and walk on."

So they continued until the husband and wife came to the Holy Scroll, and she swore, saying:

"Behold, I swear on this Book that from the day that you, my husband, went away on business, no man has touched me except the man who helped me when I fell in the mud."

And the husband believed her and they returned to the house.

There once was a very wise man and he set out to write down the wiles of women, and he gathered up many books filled with their cunning. Then he thought that there remained no cunning for him to write down.

Now he came to a certain city and he found that the governor of that city had made a banquet for all the inhabitants of the city. When the governor saw that he had come from a distant land and that he was ill, he brought him to his house and said to his wife:

"Quickly, attend him! Perhaps you can get him to eat something!"

The governor then went away with his men to the banquet, and the woman asked him: "Whence have you come?"

And he said to her: "I have gone forth to gather and to indite all the wiles of women. And I have written them all down."

Then the woman said to him: "Leave all that. See now, here we are, just the two of us, in one house, and there is no stranger with us. Come and lie with me, for my husband has taken another woman besides me."

And she began to hug and to kiss him and he arose and got onto the bed in order to lie with her. Then she screamed a tremendous scream. And her husband came, his men with him. Then the man dropped like a corpse from fear.

Said she to her husband: "Lo, you brought me a man and as soon as he started eating the food he choked and he could not swallow a thing on account of his wretched illness. So I screamed as loud as I could because I was afraid he would die."

And her husband said to her: "Give him honey to drink, but feed it to him very, very slowly."

Then the governor and his men went to the banquet. And the woman said to the wise man: "Have you written down this kind of cunning?"

And he said, "No." And he got up and he burned all his books, saying, "I have labored in vain."

PART II.
Memoirs

Give her the fruit of her hands
and let her own words praise her in the gates.
PROVERBS 31:31

�֍

Gluckel's Missing Jew

About this time [1687] a wonderful incident occurred. There lived in Altona a man, Abraham Metz by name, may God avenge his blood! He was married to my kinswoman Sarah, daughter of Elijah Cohen.* Before he moved to Hamburg he had lived in Herford and was married to the daughter of Leib Herford. She died two years after the marriage, and he then moved to Hamburg and married Sarah. He brought with him a fortune of 3000 reichstaler. But he was a stranger here and knew nothing of the manners and the business ways of the Hamburgers and within a few years had lost his entire fortune. He was a money-changer and lived at that time in Altona.

One morning his wife came into town and asked all her friends whether her husband had stayed the night at any of their houses; but after innumerable enquiries found no one with whom he had stayed. She was greatly alarmed. Many said she had quarrelled with him and he had run away from her. It was three years to the time of the incident of which I am now writing, and nothing more was heard of this Abraham Metz. Everyone had his own opinion and said just what he liked.

From *Gluckel of Hamelyn*, written by herself. Tr. Beth-Zion Abrahams, 1st American ed. 1963 NY: Thomas Yoseloff. Reprinted with permission of the publisher.
*Elijah Cohen, died 1653, was married to Glückel's aunt, her mother's sister.

Many spoke evil of him, which I do not care to repeat, or mention in connection with such a martyr—God avenge his blood! But unfortunately, human weakness is such that we speak with our mouths of what our eyes have not seen. For three years this poor Sarah was a "living widow"* alone with her sad orphans and had to allow people to talk as they would and say what they liked of her husband.

There was in the Hamburg community an honest man who, although he was not rich, supported his wife and four children quite comfortably. He was a money-changer. Every money-changer rushes around all day for his living, and towards evening, at the time of afternoon prayers, goes home and thence to synagogue. Each one belongs to a *chevra*** and with the other members studies, and after studying returns home. It was very late on this particular night when the wife waited for her husband's return from the *chevra* so that they could have their supper together. Her waiting was in vain. She ran to all their friends' houses, but could not find him. He was, through our sins, sad to tell, lost.

The next day there were rumours flying about the town. One said he had seen him here, the other that he had seen him somewhere else. At midday they spoke of it on the Börse. Zanvil the son of Reb Meyer Hekscher related, "Yesterday a woman came up to me and asked whether I had 600 or 700 reichstaler with me; if I had I should go with her—a distinguished stranger was in her house and had much gold and precious stones to sell. But I had no cash and so did not go with her." As he finished saying this a man named Lipman who stood near asked him what sort of a person she was and what

---

*A woman whose husband is missing and his fate unknown.
**A small group meeting for the purpose of study; each *chevra* studying a different subject, but all dealing with the Bible and Talmud. A *chevra* is known by the name of the subject studied.

she wore. Zanvil answered, "She wore this and that." Upon which Lipman said, "I know the woman! and also know whom she serves. I do not trust her master. Good cannot come of it." And with such talk they left the Börse, everyone going to his own house.

When Lipman reached home, he said to his wife, "Do you know what I am going to tell you? The woman who is a servant of the son of the owner of the Mariners' Tavern went to Zanvil Hekscher and would have taken him with her if he had had 600 or 700 reichstaler on him. I am sore afraid that the man who is missing went with her and has been murdered." Upon this his wife beat her hands on her head, and cried, "Through our sins! I've just remembered: the same person was also here and wanted you or me to go with her. You know very well what an evil man her master is; he is a murderer; it is certain that the upright, pious man was killed in her house." The woman, who was very capable, continued, "I will not rest or be still until I bring the whole thing to light."

"Mad woman!" cried her husband. "If it is true, what are we to do? We are in Hamburg and dare not utter a word."* So, things remained as they were for some days. However, with beat of the drum the town council proclaimed that anyone who knew anything of the missing Jew, dead or alive, should come forward and say what he knew: he would receive 100 ducats reward and his name would be kept secret. But no one came forward and the matter was soon forgotten, in the usual way. However worthy, if nothing follows, it is forgotten. But the "living widow" and her orphans remained bereaved.

It happened that one early Sabbath morning in the summer Lipman's wife could not sleep, just as once

---

*As Jews with no residential rights they lived in Hamburg on sufferance.

happened to the King of Spain. He once asked a Jewish scholar, "What is the meaning of the verse, *Hineh lo yonum v'lo yishon shomer Yisroël*?" The scholar translated, "The guardian of Israel neither slumbers nor sleeps." The King answered "That is not what it means. The real meaning is that God is the guardian Who does not let others sleep or slumber. Had I slept as usual this night you would all have been lost as a result of a blood-libel. But the Lord who is your guardian made me unable to sleep and I saw how a child was thrown into a Jewish house. Had I not been witness of this, all Jews would have been put to death."

In the same way Lipman's wife was unable to sleep. Early in the morning she stood at her window. She lived in the Ellern Steinway,** a passageway through which everyone going in or out of Altona had to pass.

It was on Friday night that she could not sleep and drove everyone mad. Her husband reproached her, asking what sort of a game this was; she would really become crazy. But she answered that nothing would help her as long as the murder was unavenged, for she knew quite well, her heart told her, that *that* man was the murderer.

Day dawned and she still stood at the window looking out on to the street. And there she saw the man whom she took to be the murderer, his wife and a servant, carrying a large box, go by. When she saw this, she cried out, "O God, stand now by me! This is the beginning of my satisfaction!" She rushed and straightway snatched up her apron and rain-cloak and ran out of the room. Her husband sprang from his bed to restrain her, but could do nothing. She ran after those people, followed them to Altona, to the river Elbe, and saw them place the box upon the bank. Rebekah, for this was her name,

---

**Old Stoneway.

decided that the corpse of the murdered man was in this box.

She ran to the people of Altona and begged them, for God's sake, to help her; she knew for certain who was the murderer. But they were unwilling and said, "It is easy to begin anything, but one cannot foretell the end." But she insisted that they should go to the President with her and at length two householders went with her. They appeared before the President and told him everything. He said to them: "If you cannot prove your accusation I will confiscate your goods and chattels." Rebekah would not allow herself to be turned aside by this, but answered, that she not only risked her property but her blood as well. "I beg you, for God's sake, Herr President, send for the murderer and take him with all that he has with him."

Upon this watchmen and soldiers were sent to the Elbe. But they arrived just in time to see them go on board ship for Harburg, an hour's journey from Altona. If they reached Harburg they would be free, for Harburg was under other jurisdiction. But the soldiers arrived in time and took the murderer together with his wife and box and brought them before the President, who ordered the box to be opened. Naught but the clothes of the murderer and his wife were found!

The fear and anxiety that fell on the poor Jews can be imagined! The man was closely examined and questioned but would confess nothing. On the contrary, he used threats and terror fell on every Jew, for he came of a large, well-known family in Hamburg. All fled in fear, but Rebekah kept saying, "I beg you, dear folk, do not despair, you will see how God will help us." In her great anxiety she ran from Altona to town. As she came into the field between Altona and Hamburg, she came face to face with the woman who was in the murderer's service. Rebekah recognized her; she was the one who had gone to the sons of Israel asking which one had about 700 reichstaler and taken him to her master's house. Rebekah went up to her and said, "It is lucky for you and your master and his wife that you have met me. They are both imprisoned in Altona for the murder they have committed. They have confessed everything, only your confession is missing. When you have confessed there is a ship waiting for you and your master and mistress to sail away in. For we Jews are only eager to know that Abraham is dead, so that his wife can marry again. We want nothing else of you."

She spoke more to the woman, for Rebekah was very clever and persuasive. Because of her words, the woman too began to talk and told her everything: how she had met Abraham on the Börse after she had called on Rebekah's husband Reb Lipman and other Jews. But no one else was so unlucky as Reb Abraham when, to his undoing, he had a full purse on him. She had shown him a small gold chain and told him that an officer in her master's house had much gold and diamonds to sell. "So Abraham came with me and when he entered the house, his slaughter-bench was ready. My master led him down to his room and together we took his life. We buried him under the threshold." Then the woman added, "Rebekah, I am telling you all this in confidence. Do not betray me." Rebekah answered her, "Are you a fool? Don't you know my honest heart? Everything I do is for your master and mistress, so that they may be soon released and out of Altona. As soon as you tell all this before our people, everything will be all right."

So the servant went to the house of the President with Rebekah. He heard out the former, and though now she stammered, repenting what she had said, still, everything was out. Most important of all, she had already revealed the burial place of the murdered man. In the end, she confessed everything to the President as she had to Rebekah. After this he again examined the master and mistress, separately, but they denied everything and said, "All that the maid has told, the hussy has herself invented." Fear again fell on us. The President said to us, "I can help you no further. Shall I torture these two on the bare word of their servant? And if he does not confess on the rack, what then? You must see to your rights in Hamburg and as soon as possible you must get permission from the Council there to search the house for the corpse. If you find it, as the maid says, you can leave the rest to me."

The *parnassim* immediately got busy and tried to get hold of twenty soldiers to dig the place that the maid had mentioned. They obtained permission to bury the corpse, if it was found, in the Jewish cemetery in Altona. At the same time they were told: "Take care: if the corpse is not found, you will be in great danger. You know the Hamburg mob! It will be impossible for us to restrain them."

We were all in great danger, but Rebekah was all over the place, and told us not to despair; she knew for certain that the corpse would be found, for the maid had sworn on her own life and had given her full particulars. Ten trusted men and several sailors who were known for their trustworthiness went, in God's name, into the murderer's house which was not far from Alten Schragen—the old shambles.

Meanwhile the news had spread in the town, and all sorts of workmen and canaille in countless numbers gathered before the door of the murderer's house. The mob had decided, "If the Jews find the murdered man, it will be well for them. If not, there will not remain a Jewish claw." But the Holy One, blessed be He, did not leave us long in doubt. As soon as our people entered the house and dug up the threshold they found what they sought. Tears filled their eyes while joy filled their hearts. They wept that such a fine pious young man, only twenty-four years old, was found in such tragic circumstances and on the other hand rejoiced that the

Community was out of danger and that vengeance was near. The whole town council was summoned and the corpse shown them and also the place where it had been found, all according to the maid's statement. The Council registered and attested this. The corpse was then placed on a wagon and brought to Altona. A multitude of sailors and apprentices was present. The sight was indescribable; perhaps there were a hundred thousand people present but not one bad word was uttered. Though they are a rough people and in quiet times we suffer much harm and distress through them, still this time everything passed off quietly and each person went his way peacefully.

The day after the *parnassim* brought the attestation to the President of Altona, who had the murderer within his jurisdiction. The Jews preferred that judgement should be given in Altona. Again he had the murderer brought before him and informed him of what had occurred. On this he made a full confession. The widow received a part of the money of her murdered husband, which was still there. The murderer, poor thing, was in prison till the time of his trial.

Meanwhile Sarah was still a "living widow". No news of her husband was to be had, and, as already related, there were many rumours. After this new murder, when everyone knew the murderer so well, it was remembered that before he moved into the house near the Alten Schragen, he lived with his father who owned the Mariners' Tavern, the best known inn in the whole of Hamburg. It is quite near the Börse and Jewish as well as gentile merchants who had business, or a reckoning with one another, went there and they used to drink there out of silver dishes. The son was therefore well known to Jews. When it became known that this very son was a murderer, and remembered that Sarah's husband was a money-changer, it was also remembered that the changers used to meet in that inn and do their business there, counting out money, for the place was well known for its security. Sarah knew also that her husband had been quite friendly with this son. She therefore went to her friends and said, "You know that my husband was lost a few years ago. The murder of Abraham has come to light. My husband went often in and out of that house. I believe that the same man killed my husband. Help me, perhaps we may find that my husband lost his life by the same hand."

What need have I to dwell long on this? They went to the President and put this before him. He spoke to the murderers with good and bad words, threatened them with torture, to confess that he had killed Abraham Metz. For long he would not confess and only agreed that he had known him well. But the President spoke so long to him until he confessed that he had killed Abraham Metz in the Mariners' Tavern. He had buried him in a deep hole in the room kept only for cheeses and filled it up with lime before closing it up.

As soon as this was known, the *parnassim* went to the Hamburg Council and as before asked permission to make a search. Again Jews were in dire peril, worse than before, that such a well-esteemed and distinguished house should be turned into a den of murderers. It was dangerous in case the corpse should not be found. Luckily for us it was found; he still wore his red under-waistcoat with silver buttons and *arbakanfos*.* He also was given Jewish burial.

There was great mourning in our community, as though they had been killed that day. The friends of my kinswoman Sarah, before they allowed the burial, examined the corpse well, for Sarah told of certain marks on his body that might be known for certain that he was indeed her dead husband and that she was really widowed. These were found and she had permission to

---

*undergarment with tassels (tsitsit).

marry again. After this the result of the trial was made known: the murderer was to be broken at the wheel and his body, bound round with iron bands, placed on a stake, that he should be an example for a long time. His wife and servant were freed, but had to leave the country. On the day of the trial and sentence there was a great tumult in Hamburg; for more than a hundred years no trial had caused such a sensation. Jews were in dire peril, for hatred for them was roused, but God in His great mercy did not forget us that day. So this too passed without harm to Jews.

✳

The Debate

(Here is a debate between Ernestine L. Rose and Horace Mann, Feb. 1852, which never took place. It is based on the statements attributed to Horace Mann which were published in his lectures. When this was published by Ernestine Rose, Mann cited it as an example of criticism of his views by "a distinguished advocate of woman's rights.")

H. M.:   The human soul and feelings were created male and female as much as their bodies ... The structure is entirely different in the sexes; there is not one single organ in structure, position and function alike in man and woman, and therefore there can be no equality between the sexes.

E. R.:   Suppose, then, that the structure of the sexes is different—that the heart, lungs, liver, stomach, or any other of the organs requisite in the human economy are larger, smaller, situated a sixteenth of an inch higher, or lower, more to the right or the left, in man or woman, what then? Does it follow that woman cannot, or must not be socially, civilly, and politically his equal?

H. M.:   As well might knives and forks, hooks and eyes,

© *Ernestine L. Rose: Women's Rights Pioneer* by Yuri Suhl, 2nd Edition, 1990, © Biblio Press, N.Y.

buttons and button-holes claim equality as man and woman.

E. R.: I will not presume to comment on this philosophical simile, it being the product of the "higher intellect of the sterner sex . . ."

H. M.: It is the woman has been oppressed and degraded by man, and it is not to be wondered at; when we see her run to the extravagance of calling conventions, and under the banner of woman's rights appear on the forum and make speeches, she unsexes herself and loses the grace and delicacy of her sex, and gains none of the superior powers of the other.

E. R.: That is as modest as it is consistent. He admits woman is oppressed and degraded by man, but to claim and vindicate her right to call conventions and appear on the forum where she would have a chance to be heard then "she unsexes herself," etc. . . . But what does the Honorable Lawgiver really mean by that term? I fear we will have to send it to Washington for congressional deliberation.

H. M.: What have been the rank and influence of woman for 6,000 years? Man has immensely degraded her; she has been little more than the mother of a race—such a race! that it might be doubted if its increase would be a benefit to the world.

E. R.: What else, Mr. Lecturer, *could* have been the rank and influence of woman than to be the mother of just *such* a race, bad as it may be, judging from some specimens, when she has been "immensely oppressed and degraded by man?"

H. M.: For four thousand years the Jewish women did

nothing but give birth to a race of unmerciful, stiff-necked men.

E. R.: . . . unmerciful and stiff-necked as the Jews are they still are the authors and originators of his religion, and a Jewish woman was the mother of his Redeemer. Well, gratitude is a virtue; and seeing how corrupt the race is, it is quite refreshing to find one mother's son possessing the amiable virtue of gratitude to God's (His God's) chosen people.

H. M.: Joan of Arc commanded an army but she brought her sword back pure without a bloodstain, still the best place for woman is at home with her family; for a man to take care of children would be like an elephant hatching chickens.

E. R.: Perhaps if woman had more to command, fewer swords would be stained with human blood, until they finally might be made into plowshares.

H. M.: . . . The greatest pride of woman should be as a housekeeper, as a scientific cook, to enable her to cook a good breakfast, and keep it nice and hot till her husband is ready for it, to take care of the wardrobe, and keep the buttons where they belong; but her greatest duty is at the cradle, to take care and educate the children.

E. R.: If men and women were educated in accordance with their predilections and tastes, it might so happen that some men might have the best capacity for the science of cooking and some women for the science of government. And as for "buttons," every girl ought to know how to sew on buttons, and I am quite willing to give the same privilege to men, particularly to the bachelors. But the lecturer can certainly not insist that . . . the Creator assigned the wardrobe to woman, for according to the Bible, "Did the Lord God make coats of skins buttons and all and clothed them?"

Genesis iii 21

H. M.: The law is not at all suited for woman. She lacks that hard, dry, calculating spirit . . . she lacks the unflinching nerve demanded in a judge, the endurance required in a juror.

E. R.: That the law is a dry subject I doubt not; but seeing how soft most lawyers are it does not appear to require a very hard head to master it, though it may require a very hard heart to carry it out . . . Has the lecturer ever found a woman flinch from a trying position? Let him point her out, and she will be as great a curiosity as his arguments.

H. M.: Fancy to yourself one husband's wife locked up in the jury room with another's wife's husband and see them marching two and two after the court martial to and from the jury room.

E. R.: Let him remember—*Honi soit qui mal y pense!**
The lecturer, I ask pardon, was not as wise as a certain mayor of a country town who, on apologizing to a prince who visited the town, for not firing cannons, gave eighteen reasons; the first was, the town had no cannons with which reason the prince was so well satisfied that he dispensed with the other seventeen. Had we had the last of the above series of reasons first we might with royal magnanimity have saved the lecturer the trouble of giving, and us of hearing the other seventeen.

H. M.: Politics! politics! that any person could ever wish to see woman embarked upon this Stygian lake, is incomprehensible! . . . the political and

---

*Evil to him who has evil thoughts

legislative bear-garden ... [is] the deepest and darkest sink of corruption, and hence woman ought not to have anything to do with government.

E. R.: I have not the least idea of disputing the lecturer's opinion on government, particularly as he can speak from personal experience. But that such a description would have the effect to reassure and satisfy woman that she is quite safe in leaving her best and dearest interests in the hands of such a "set of animals" is rather doubtful, particularly as it might suggest itself to her mind that as the government is in such a lamentable, disgraceful condition would it not be well, even as a mere experiment, to send these legislative gentlemen home to be tamed, and let women take their places.

✳

Justice, Justice!

In July, 1892, Emma Goldman and her companion, Alexander Berkman, called "Sasha," decided to express, by a "propaganda action" as anarchists, their response to Henry Clay Frick. He was head of the Carnegie Steel Corp., Pittsburgh. He had evicted from their factories and homes strikers and their families and used armed Pinkerton guards against them. With $40. Emma gave Sasha, he bought dynamite and attempted to make a bomb. (It was tested and failed to go off, however) Here, Emma expresses her solidarity with him:

"I will go with you, Sasha," I cried; "I must go with you! I know that as a woman I can be of help. I could gain access to Frick easier than you. I could pave the way for your act. Besides, I simply must go with you. Do you understand, Sasha?"

We have a feverish week. Sasha's experiments took place at night when everybody was asleep. While Sasha worked, I kept watch. I lived in dread every moment for Sasha, for our friends in the flat, the children, and the rest of the tenants. What if anything should go wrong—but, then, did not the end justify the means? Our end was the sacred cause of the oppressed and exploited people. It was for them that we were going to

From Emma Goldman, *Living My Life*, New York: Alfred A. Knopf, Inc., 1931.

give our lives. What if a few should have to perish?—
the many would be made free and could live in beauty
and in comfort. Yes, the end in this case justified the
means.*

*But many years later—in 1930, when Emma wrote her auto-
biography, she came to a different conclusion:*

It was my religiously devout belief that the end justi-
fies all means. The end, then, was my ideal of human
brotherhood. If I have undergone any change it is not
in my ideal. It is more in the realization that a great
end does not justify *all* means.

* * *

*Emma Goldman's powerful sense of justice is here evident
from her mother's example:*

Whenever I visited Rochester, Mother had new con-
quests to report. For years the orthodox Jews of the city
had discussed the need of an orphanage and a home
for the indigent aged. Mother did not waste words; she
located two sites, purchased them on the spot, and for
months canvassed the Jewish neighbourhood for contri-
butions to pay off the mortgage and build the institu-
tions the others had only talked about. There was no
prouder queen than Mother on the opening day of the
new orphanage. She invited me to "come and speak a
piece" on the great occasion. I had once told her that
my aim was to enable the workers to reap the fruit of
their labours, and every child to enjoy our social
wealth. A mischievous twinkle had come into her still
sparkling eyes as she replied: "Yes, my daughter, that
is all very good for the future; but what is to become of
our orphans now, and the old and decrepit who are

alone in the world? Tell me that." And I had no answer to give.

One of her exploits had been to put the Rochester manufacturer of shrouds out of business because of exorbitant charges. The owner of the business, a woman, had a monopoly of furnishing the burial garments without which no orthodox Jew may be laid to final rest. An old woman of the poorest class needed a shroud, but her family could not pay the high price asked for it. When my mother learned of it, she at once proceeded in her usual energetic manner. She called on the heartless creature who had enriched herself on the dead, and demanded that the garment be supplied at once without pay, threatening to ruin her in case of refusal. The manufacturer remained unmoved, and my mother set to work forthwith. She bought white material and with her own hands made a shroud for the pauper; then she called on the largest dry-goods store in the city and succeeded in convincing the owner of the riches he would store up in heaven if he would sell the material in quantities at cost price. "Anything for you, Mrs. Goldman," the man had said, Mother reported proudly. Then she organized a group of Jewish women to sew the shrouds, and she made it known in the community that the garments would be furnished for ten cents apiece. The clever scheme brought about the bankruptcy of the monopolist.

❁

Votes for Women

One Sabbath afternoon all we young people assembled in the house of a favourite young married couple to discuss affairs from our own point of view, which, naturally enough, was not always approved of by our elders. After a while we got on to the question of the "emancipation of women," which was already in the air. Now we girls had talked it over already among ourselves, but to-day the young men were present too, and they declared that in principle it was all very well, indeed quite right, that women should have their say in communal matters, but they would have to be prepared for having a vote by quite a different system of education. This was always a sore point, because most of the young men had studied and passed their High School or University examinations, but several of the girls had also attended a high school in Russia, but had been shut out from the Universities by the Russian "percentage" and had managed, often at great sacrifice on their own and their parents' part, to go to Switzerland, Paris, or Berlin, and complete their studies there. Others had come with their families to Palestine, leaving an uncompleted school course behind them, and these were the most persistent of all in the matter of the vote, because they were suffering, so they felt, from a double injustice:

From *Pioneers in Palestine* by Hannah Trager (1870–1943), © E. P. Dutton & Co., NY, 1925.

—— 59 ——

they might not have a vote because they had not obtained a degree, and this degree they had been prevented from obtaining. "Well," said one of the young fellows pulling a paper out of his pocket, "you girls will like this," and he read aloud an article on the women of America, telling how they were not only insisting on their "rights" but were, in a fair way to obtain them sooner or later.

"Then why is it," exclaimed a girl when he had finished, "that American women go forward and we Jewish women stick in one place?"

"Look at the old days when the daughters of Zelophehad stood up for themselves and claimed their inheritance. Look at Deborah, without whom the leader of the Israelites refused to go out to battle. Look at Judith, look at the many Jewish women of Biblical times who had as much wisdom and courage as the men. Tell me, is it right that we should be treated as if we were only fit to agree to anything that is decided by the men?"

"And now," broke in another girl "is the time for us colony women to take a stand for our fair share in communal matters. Here we are, helping to build up a new commonwealth in a country where we are all really free to do as we like. Are we going to build on a basis of equality or not? Have not we women taken our part in the founding of this colony as fully as the men have? Did not our mothers suffer and struggle as well as our fathers? Have we girls ever refused to help in any kind of work, indoors or out? Have we not weeded in the vineyards in the burning sun, and made the hay, and milked the cows? Have we not done our best in times of sickness and trouble? Are you afraid that we shall fail you in the future? Let us go forward together, not struggling against one another, and if our parents see that you young men are for us they will begin to look at the whole question with different eyes."

"They are quite right," said one young man after the

other, more astonished at this eloquence on a girl's part than they quite liked to confess, while we girls glowed with satisfaction, but at the same time thought it wiser not to say too much just then. One of them, however, remarked,

"We shall count on your help at the next *vaad** meeting, when we are going to bring the question of our vote forward," said the first girl.

"Good," said the young men, "we are on your side and will do what we can."

The next thing for the girls was to talk their mothers over, and persuade them into taking up with the idea of "women's rights." Most of the mothers thought it newfangled nonsense, and told the girls, that once they were married, they would have quite enough to do without interfering in the management of the colony. The girls, however, explained to them that nothing stood still, that new times were coming when it would be up to the women to see their own daughters treated as they should be, and two or three girls even spoke to their fathers who said neither yes nor no, but discussed it with their wives in the daughters' absence and found them already taking the girls' view.

When the day for the *vaad** came round everyone went who could, even some young wives with babies in their arms, some to speak for or against, and some to see the fun.

The question was brought up at the end of the meeting, and laid before the Elders of the Colony. They were very angry, and when the young men kept their word and stood up for women having a voice in affairs, it made matters no better.

"What next will you be introducing from America?" they asked. "Strikes perhaps. We do not want such things in a Jewish Colony in the Holy Land."

---

*committee or council

"What we want in our colonies," returned the young men, "is the old Jewish spirit of liberty and justice, and not the narrow spirit of bigotry and the oppression of the weaker, from which we ourselves have suffered so much and which we have learnt to detest. Go back to the history of the days of old, and see what the Jewish woman could do when she was given the chance. And what about our women in times of persecution, in the days of the Romans? In the days of the Crusades? Were they behind the men in courage, in intelligence, in devotion? Were they spared by the Inquisition? And now that we are not in the Middle Ages, are we to be narrower and more prejudiced than our forefathers were in the days of old?"

"Let us hear what the older women have to say, if you will not listen to us young folk," said one.

Then some of the mothers spoke, and a few were antipathetic, declaring that their daughters were quite independent enough as it was, thinking themselves superior to their own mothers, but most were sympathetic and said that although they themselves had no wish to interfere in communal affairs, they wanted their children and grandchildren to "come into their own," and to be like Miriam, Deborah, Huldah, and the five daughters of Zelophehad, of whom they had lately heard so much.

At last the elders said they would think it over, and it should be brought up for fresh discussion on some future occasion. But the girls had foreseen the probability of this, (having learnt by former experiences of the kind) and demanded a decision in their favour there and then. And they had their way.

There was great clapping of hands and the young folk left the hall singing, so that even the elders smiled grimly into their beards.

*

Hunger

I would like to tell about Joseph Mattes, who devoted himself to religious matters while his wife sold geese. Even before the German occupation, the cost of a goose had risen to twenty-five rubles. Who on Krochmalna Street could afford such luxury? Joseph Mattes, his wife, daughters, and their husbands had been left penniless. While other goose dealers had managed to put something aside, Joseph Mattes had given his whole fortune to charity and the Radzymin Rabbi.

The extent of his poverty was not known by those in the study house, and besides, the war had intensified individual selfishness. Men with full pantries worshipped alongside those who had nothing, but seldom thought of helping them. There wasn't actually that much food to share. Fear of the future haunted everyone. No one any longer thought the war would end soon.

I became personally acquainted with hunger, and I noticed that the skin hung loosely on Joseph Mattes's pale face. But his son-in-law, Israel Joshua, was even paler and more emaciated. The young man, tugging at a barely sprouting beard, hovered over the holy books, sighing and stealing glances beyond them. The delicate young man suffered from shame as well. He yearned to

From *In My Father's Court: A Memoir* by Isaac Bashevis Singer. © Farrar, Straus & Giroux, NY *1962*. Reprinted with permission of the publisher.

serve the Almighty, but hunger tormented him. Sinking ever more deeply into the Hasidic books, he twisted his sidelocks incessantly. What could he do about it, I wondered, this son-in-law living on his father-in-law's bounty and starving? Timid and weak, prematurely round-shouldered, he could do nothing but study and pray, and look into the *Grace of Elimelech* or *The Holiness of Levi*. . . .

One Friday evening, Joseph Mattes, who had given his fortune toward Hasid banquets and the support of the Radzymin Rabbi, slammed his fist on the table, shouting, "Men, I don't have the bread to usher in the Sabbath!"

His words were an indication of the times. Bread had had to be substituted for the Sabbath wine when making the benediction.

For a moment there was silence, and after that, tumult, confusion. Reb Joseph's sons retreated into corners, dreadfully ashamed of what their father had said. Israel Joshua became chalk-white. Despite the collection of bread, fish, and Sabbath loaves that was taken up that night, nothing, essentially changed. Paupers remained paupers, and benefactors were few. I felt terribly afraid the same thing might happen to my father.

Like most of the Rabbis, the Radzymin Rabbi had moved to Warsaw, where he owned property. He was reputedly wealthy, but this was dubious, since real estate had ceased to provide income. I do not know whether he helped the Hasidim or not. Nevertheless, we were so much in need that Father paid a visit to the Radzymin Rabbi's wife—who was partially responsible for my father's loss of position as head of the yeshivah. This so-called "young Rebbetzin," however, was not to be envied, for even though medical opinion blamed her husband for their lack of children, the Rabbi insisted it was his wife's fault and demanded a divorce. Although she did not object to a divorce, the Rebbetzin asked a

25,000 ruble settlement, which the Rabbi was unwilling to pay. He was constantly tormenting and disgracing her, she told Father, taking her to Wonder Rabbis and doctors, refusing to give her sufficient household money. Unable to lend Father anything, she begged him to accept her diamond ring and pawn it. Father protested, but the Rebbetzin swore: "By my life and health, take it!" showing him, at the same time, a Talmudic passage that prohibited the wearing of jewelry while others starved.

When Father in his shame returned home carrying the ring in a box, Mother made a face, perhaps from jealousy. But when Father pawned the ring, we bought flour, bread, and groats. Meat was too expensive. We began to use cocoa butter, which could be eaten with both meat and milk dishes.

✽

Two Encounters

For the past twenty-five years, whenever we were in town, Miss Brenauer, the milliner of Beekman Place has hardly ever missed making a Friday morning telephone call to wish me a good Sabbath. These calls are precious to me.

I was always proud and happy to feel that we could afford to buy for our daughters the lovely hats that Miss Brenauer conceived and fashioned. But Miss Brenauer to me is far more than hats. She is a link with my departed youth, a signpost of age that I cherish equally, and an overture to the Sabbath eve which, with ceremony or without (without ceremony these bedridden days), is always an event for me.

Speaking of hats makes me think of one time when I was not true to Miss Brenauer. That was the time when I met Mrs. James Roosevelt, the President's mother. It was at the home of Mrs. Henry Morgenthau, Jr. When I was introduced to her she said, "I don't like your hat." She said I simply must go for my next hat to her milliner, "a wonderful little woman," and she gave me a note to her milliner, telling her to do her best for me. Her paeans of praise induced me to go to her "wonderful little woman," who did proceed to do her best for me.

The next time I was due to meet Mrs. Roosevelt, I put

From *More Yesterdays, An Autobiography (1925–1949)* by Rebekah Kohut. Reprinted with permission. Bloch Publishing Co. 1950 on this new creation. Mrs. Roosevelt, when she saw me, said, "I don't like your hat. You simply must go to my milliner." I said nothing about this headpiece being the exact result of her counsel, but I had much inward amusement. Then there was another meeting at Mrs. Morgenthau's at which Mrs. Roosevelt was expected, and this time I was determined to wear one of my best Brenauers. Mrs. Roosevelt was delighted with my hat, and said, "Now that is really something. Aren't you glad you went to my milliner?" She was so pleased, in fact, that, upon leaving, she asked me to run up to her house with her and have some sandwiches. Well, we had already had sandwiches where we were, but I went with her and we had some more (and very good, too).

*   *   *

One of my best friends is Martha McGee. Martha is eight years old. Her father was superintendent of the apartment house where I have lived during all of my illness. Martha was brought to my bedside when she was three weeks old, and ever since we have been great friends. As she grew up a little table and chair were placed for her in my room, and she played there with her toys, ate there frequently, and to her I was Grandma Kohut. She played constantly in the room while I had visitors, and she often took part in the conversation and made comments on my visitors after they were gone.

Martha's family moved to New Jersey two years ago, and so I only see her on special occasions when she is brought to New York. She flatteringly misjudges my influence. She paid me a visit one St. Patrick's Day and told me she was going to the parade and would sit next to President Truman on the reviewing stand. I asked her how that was going to be arranged, and to her it was very simple. She was going to tell the policemen that she was Mrs. Kohut's grandchild, and they would, of course, find a place for her next to the President.

Another time, when she visited me, I asked her how she liked New Jersey. She said, "It's all right, but there's too many Jew women there." I was distressed to realize that this lovely child with so much genuine heart and sweetness in her was already picking up wisps of anti-Semitic hate in the air and that prejudice, unbeknownst, was entering her soul and was on the way to blighting what was meant to be a splendid person. I think I dispelled that. I said that was not a nice way to talk about the people of the mother of Jesus, also a Jewish woman, and that I and many people she had met in my house since her infancy, and whom she loved and who loved her, were Jews. It surprised and troubled her, and she turned it over much in her little head. I explained what prejudice was, how it grew, and how it twisted and distorted people who could have been the finest, most loving creatures. I never heard such remarks from her again.

�֍

Honeymoon and Conflicts

My lover was a Doctor of Philosophy and twenty-seven, and I a staid social worker, a Bachelor of Arts and twenty-two, but the education of our time had not thought it necessary to teach two young people how to be man and wife.

For a little while we were just brother and sister, only clinging close to one another, seeking one another. It may seem curious, but this is just as it was with us.

Then we bought an old medical book and read about marriage, and made our marriage solemn and complete. It is strange that so much has been written about the love of men and women not married, and so little of the love of man and wife!

We were young, and we were well. We were mysterious and beautiful to one another. I had, all my life, thought of the womanhood in me as something rather to be deprecated; a man, I knew, of my faith, must absent himself from his wife, as from defilement, at certain holy times of his life. And always, she must humbly beg God to pardon her that she is a woman. Had I not read, in the prayer book, the words my brothers, my father, all my uncles, spoke daily—thanking God they were not women?

From *I Am A Woman And A Jew* by Leah Morton (pseud. Elizabeth Gertrude Stern), J.H. Sears & Co., NY 1926, reprinted with permission of Markus Weiner Publishing, NY, 1986.

But my love found me God-worthy because I was a woman. He found me holy.

Of children we did not speak. At that time birth control was not a word spoken. There was a sin called preventing the conception of children, but Margaret Sanger had not yet appeared. Girls became pregnant and had abortions.

But married women had as many children as fate chose. If they were much advanced they might live only at certain times with their husbands, and have protection against pregnancy so. That was mentioned, in an awed whisper, by prurient-minded, but kindly, married women, to young brides.

I did not know whether I wanted to be a wife, living in my husband's love, or a woman building her career.

My husband was modern. He said I must do anything I wanted to do, just as he did what he chose. Only, he added, *he* must earn our living. Whatever *I* did I could do without thinking whether it was successful or not; only whether it made me happy.

I took his hands in mine, I recall, and put his palms against my cheek. But he did not feel how hot my cheeks were against his palms. I kissed him But as I kissed him then, I know I wished he had said that my work was as *practically* a need to me, as his—that it was as essential to our life as his. If work was to be judged by him by its practical value to his life and mine, I would have wanted him to see that which I chose to do, too, as practical, and helpful as his own.

He thought I might do social work as a volunteer, without pay.

I was, however, determined not to do that, not to be an amateur. I wanted to work just as he did. I would not be happy otherwise, I told him.

He took me on his knee then, kissed me, and told me I was a violent feminist. But he liked it in me, I knew. In fact, he was, himself, in his quiet way a feminist, too. I had been a member of a committee to arrange a meeting for Anna Howard Shaw, and when she came, he did the then striking thing of standing at the door of the little hall and greeting each person as she came in—for alas, only one other man came. I did not go with the suffrage party to Washington on any of its trips, but I saved money from lunches, and sent it to them anonymously.

"So you want a career," he smiled, "and a husband tacked on?"

It was a striking thing, but I said, seriously, "Haven't you one with me tacked on?"

He kissed me then, and laughed, very tenderly indeed.

＊

I Fight for My Mother (1928–1932)

My mother at this time was in the state hospital in Binghamton, New York. I used to visit her once a month. She, as you know, had attempted suicide again. My father had committed her. And this, I tell you, is the story of the first victory I won. If you understand this story you understand my life. And why? Because this time my mother was in there for good. My father was her guardian, that's how it was. He certainly didn't want her home again. Over her life he had complete power. He didn't love her. Did I say love? He never even liked her. From the moment we put down our feet in America with his two fists he began to destroy her. Then, he tried to run from her. Now, without paying, he saw a way to be rid of her for good.

Binghamton Hospital was such a place, if you had an enemy, still you wouldn't put him there. No, I tell you, if this enemy was so bad milk would curdle because he came near to it, still you wouldn't put him there. I would not put even my father there.

To this day I see the place before my eyes. Those iron beds. The bare floor. On the walls, a gray color, peeling away. It was filled with forlorn, bedraggled old people. Everywhere was a feeling of despair. Poverty we knew,

from "The Fourth Story My Mother Tells," *In My Mother's House: A Daughter's Story* by Kim Chernin. Copyright © 1983 by Kim Chernin. Reprinted by permission of Ticknor & Fields/Houghton Mifflin Co. All rights reserved.

who could complain? But this was something more, it was worse. For everyone it was terrible. But for my mother it was Gehenna, a living hell. She was completely alone. There was nobody who spoke Yiddish or Russian. Every time I came there she said, "I'm going to die here. Rochele, I'm going to die."

They used to give her injections. These needles terrified her. How could she understand what they were for? Naturally, no one explained anything to her. How could they? She didn't understand English. Later, I made inquiries. I found out she was diabetic. I explained to her why they were giving the injections, but she was still afraid. Each time I came, she grabbed my hand and squeezed it: "Rochele, take me out of here."

When I came away, after a visit, I was in such a state. I didn't know what to do. At the hospital, I used to ask them if we could bring her maybe to New York City. There she could be closer to me. I could visit her every week. But they said, "She cannot be moved." Always the same thing. "You are not her guardian. You're her daughter. Only your father can give the permission for her to change to another place."

I wrote to my father, I asked him if Mama could be transferred to another hospital. Always I received the same reply: "When she gets better she will be released. Until then, what can be done?"

So, every month I went there and every month she was getting worse. She cried all the time. She had been a woman with a nice shape, but now she was so thin you thought maybe they were starving her in this place. No one combed her hair. No one dressed her. She wore one of those institutional gowns, all wrinkled.

"Rochele, I'm going to die here," was all she could say to me.

This was my mother. My mother, you understand? Maybe I sent her back to live with my father. Maybe I left her and went away into my life. But now? Could I leave her now like this, in such a place, desperate?

Finally, I couldn't live with it anymore. It was eating up my life. One time, after my visit, I was in the station. The train was coming. I was on my feet, walking to get on there. But suddenly I was running, away from the train, back to the hospital. I stormed in there, asking for the head psychiatrist.

"It's after visiting hours," the nurse said to me. But believe me, I gave her such a look, she turned right around and took me to the doctor.

"This is no place for her," I told him. He asked me to sit down. "Sit?" I said. "I should sit here while my mother is in torment?" He gives me a look. Two months before, this look maybe would get me to sit down. But now? Nothing could stop me. "Doctor," I said, "what do I know about medicine? I admit, I know nothing. Do I know what your diagnosis is? This, too, I don't know. But, Doctor, I am here to tell you, you yourself don't know if this woman is sick. You're holding her here because my father wants it that way."

"Sick?" he says. "You can see for yourself. She won't eat. She's terribly confused. The nurses talk to her. The other patients talk to her. She just doesn't respond."

Could I believe what my ears were hearing? "Doesn't respond?" Was there something wrong in this man? "Of course she doesn't respond. She can't speak English. Naturally she won't eat the food. This food is not the food she's used to. Everything here is strange to her. These aren't her people. This is what you are calling insane?"

He didn't say anything. But I remember, he wasn't looking at me. He was looking down, at the desk. So I said, "To you any foreign person would be peculiar, wouldn't they? You think she's insane because you are not used to people like her."

But now, of course, I am beginning to shake. This

man, I think to myself, is a doctor. And who am I to be talking to a doctor like this? But still, I notice that my mouth is talking. I begin to reason with him: "What would you lose if I took her home? I'm married. To an engineer. And we are willing to have her live with us."

Here he suddenly looked up. He seemed astonished. "She can't stay in a normal environment," he said. "She's insane. Suppose she killed somebody?"

My mother kill somebody? My mother? She, the most gentle creature in the world? Now my voice went up. It got louder: "Nobody said she was violent. Nobody. How could anyone say such a thing about her? The only person she tried to kill was herself."

But he insisted, "She could endanger your life. You can't take her home. Your father is her guardian. He is the only person who can remove her. And he wants her here."

Now, I ask you, what would you do in my place? I had reached the point where I couldn't live with this situation. I couldn't stand the injustice in it. That selfish old man oppressing this woman so he wouldn't have to take responsibility for her.

But what could I do? What could anyone do? Even in America my father had the law on his side. This bothered me. We had expected so much from America. I couldn't believe this old woman would be left to suffer like that. At night I would wake up shaking my pillow, squeezing and shaking it.

Then I remembered we knew a lawyer in Binghamton whose name was Chernin. He was a distant cousin. I looked up his name in the telephone book. The next time I went to visit my mother, I called this man. "You don't know me," I said. "My name is Rose Chernin. But my father always told me that Chernin, spelled like this, is from the same family."

The man was happy to speak to me. After all, we were

kinsmen. I went to see him and told him our story. "A Jewish man," he says, "treating a wife like this?"

He wanted to meet my mother, so right away I took him to the hospital. He was a cheerful man. I remember he was talking, telling his stories as we walked through the gate. But in the hospital he took one look and, let me tell you, he reached out, he grabbed my wrist. Good, I thought to myself; now he sees, he'll help us.

My mother came over. "Let me go away with you, Rochele," she said. "Take me away from here." She turned to this man. "Tell her," she said to him in Yiddish, "tell her I'll die here."

Well, I don't have to make a long story out of it. The next time I went to speak with this man he says to me, "If your husband is willing to become her guardian I think it will be possible to get her out of here."

Could I tell you how I felt? I was going to bring Mama home. I brought her a velvet dress. It was made for her specially by a woman I knew, a seamstress who was working in the ILGWU, Sonia Bloom, the sister of the famous painter. She was living downstairs from us and when I told her, "Sonia, I'm bringing Mama home," she went off and ripped down some curtains. She made a beautiful dress for Mama. We went out and bought black shoes, a little purse for her, some earrings.

The nurse brought Mama out, her hair was combed, she was wearing the velvet dress. "Mama," I said to her, "I'm taking you home. You're going home with me, Mama."

She put her hand up to her cheek. Her voice was thin. "Home," she said. "For a vacation?"

"For good, Mama," I said, throwing my arms around her. "You'll never come back here again."

So there you have it. This was the first battle I won against injustice. It made on me a deep impression. I had a sense now of what was possible. An ignorant woman could oppose a doctor. She would win against an educated man. A woman could stand up against an institution.

✳

Bobbe and Us

Like the enterprising little pig in the children's story who was forever outsmarting the wolf, Bobbe was always one step ahead of the junk man. She scavenged the gutters in our neighborhood for pop bottles so she could return them to the grocer for the two cent deposit. Oildrum trash barrels in back alleys were treasure troves to her. She was so short, I wonder now how she could see inside them, but she did and found plenty, too, to drag to the junk shop, where she let the junk man have her booty for a price.

She didn't look odd to us, but I suppose she must have been a strange sight, scarcely taller than a child, a kerchief knotted at the back of her head, barely covering thin, colorless hair and pendulous earlobes pierced by tiny brown stones. Her body was wrapped, winter and summer, in aprons and sweaters with several pairs of thick cotton stockings wrinkling on her swollen legs. She kept busy all day as she had almost all her life, buying and selling.

Her favorite scheme, though, was dealing in handkerchiefs. Fagin, had he only known her, would have made her a full partner. There was nothing dishonest in it, you understand. She only dealt in *lost* handkerchiefs,

From *A Leak in the Heart: Tales From A Woman's Life* by Faye Moskowitz. Copyright © 1985 by Faye Moskowitz. Reprinted by permission of David R. Godine, Publisher, Boston.

ones that tumbled from an ample bosom, fell out of a handbag, or came out of a back pocket when a gentleman removed his wallet.

Being my mother's child still, I was certain those bits of cloth crawled with TB and polio germs, and I told her so when I discovered what she was doing. She paid no attention, of course, and came home each afternoon, washed the handkerchiefs, pressed them, and sold them to the used clothing store. Later, when for many reasons we became intimate, she told me that the synagogue was her most lucrative haunt. After services, she might haul in four or five sodden hankies dropped by mourners in the women's section who had come to say *kaddish* for their dead.

My mother came to America in the twenties in the last of the hopeful waves of immigrants. If she ever felt oppressed in her role as a female, she never communicated it to me. I think she was far too busy adapting to the ways of her adopted country to bother with any such ideas.

When I was a child, the mothers of my friends, like my own mother, stayed home and kept house. It was hard enough for men to find work during the Depression. Married women coped with their husband's shrunken paychecks—or often no paycheck at all. They put up and let down pant cuffs and hems until the material fell apart, stretched the stew until finding the meat became a game, and sent us to school so well-scrubbed we squeaked.

No matter how little we had, my mother refused to allow us to consider ourselves in want. I remember vividly a visit to an aunt's house when I was about five years old. We all sat in the summer kitchen while my mother and her sister chattered endlessly about things that didn't interest me, and I whined and whined, complaining that I was hungry. I couldn't understand why I was offered nothing to eat or why my mother kept motioning me to be quiet. Finally my aunt said, "Sweet-heart, how about some bread and milk?"

By this time I really was hungry, and angry too, and I shouted, "Only poor people eat bread and milk."

I'll never forget my mother's face and how fiercely she said to me, "Don't you ever call us poor. We are not poor. Only people who have no hope are poor."

Poverty is no disgrace; neither is it an honor.
YIDDISH SAYING

For wisdom is better than rubies; and all the things that may be desired are not to be compared to it.

Proverbs 8:11

✳

The Strike

Coming home from school, I found my older brothers, and Mama and Papa, sitting around the table. Surprised at this unusual manner of spending a working day, I called out, "Is today some sort of holiday I forgot?"

Mama looked at me and said drily, "Yes, it's a holiday that's not in the *louach* (religious calendar). The shop is on strike!"

So Jan Pulski had kept his threat.

"Only our shop, Mama?" I asked.

"No, everyone. The whole needle trade is at a standstill. If you go into the kitchen, you'll find some cocoa on the stove. Then go up and practice like a good girl. If you wait until Sidney comes home, he'll want to practice, and you'll fight as usual. In the end neither of you will practice."

"I will, Mama, in just a little while. I have to draw something with my compass before I forget how to do it."

It wasn't really the drawing that kept me dawdling in my corner of the table. I had to know about the strike. They were discussing it, "mapping out their strategy," Abe called it.

From *Horsecars and Cobblestones* by Sophie Ruskay. © 1973 A.S. Barnes & Co., NY. Reprinted with permission for this edition by Ceil Ruskay Schatz.

"How many can we depend on to stick to us?"

"The real problem is to keep the cutting room going—how, otherwise, can we get enough bundles to the out-of-town factories?"

Papa strode up and down the room, shaking his head belligerently. "We'll see who can hold out longer, they or us."

Weeks passed, and the strike dragged on. There seemed to be no end in sight.

"Who can keep this up?" Mama complained bitterly, night after night, as she waited for Papa and the boys to come home, often guarded by a policeman. "We'll lose our business. What sense does it all make?" She shrugged her shoulders. "And the workers—God knows, if by this time they have even bread to eat!"

Each day Mama was full of hope that a settlement would be reached, only to hear the same disappointing news at night. She vented her wrath on the union organizers. "Those walking delegates, they don't want to settle. Recognize the union, that's what they want, so that they can dictate to us."

Mama had not gone to the shop for weeks. Her girls dropped in almost daily and asked to be allowed to go to work. "For you," they said, "we'll gladly go through fire."

Mama was touched and proud of their love, but she would not hear of it. "Besides," Mama confided one day to Lizzie, one of the foreladies, "we may soon give up the ladies' underwear department." Mama quickly answered the look on Lizzie's face. "You don't have to worry, nor the other girls, either. If we can't place everybody in our own shop, Jake Goldberg would kiss his ten fingers to get any of our operators. I don't have to praise myself, but you know how he feels about the girls I have trained."

That night while Papa was trying to forget his troubles in the pages of his newspaper, Mama further elaborated her ideas. She was combing my hair, while I sat on a wooden chair before her, my head still aching from the vigorous rubbing it had received.

"You know, Simon, I haven't patience anymore with the embroideries, the petticoats with their flounces, the muslin drawers, open and closed, the chemises down to the knees. Take my word for it, a change is coming in the ladies' underwear trade, as I told you before, not once, but twenty times. I'm thinking of closing the department for good. When the strike is over, we'll make room for something new—maybe a line of pajamas, men's nightgowns are not selling the way they used to either."

"Simon," Mama went on, "we'll stop making the women's underwear and make room for something new. In business you have to go backward or forward, you can't stand still."

Papa put down his newspaper. "If you ask me, the business is already going backward. To listen to you, no one would imagine that we are going through one of the worst strikes we ever had—and you talk of opening a new department."

"Believe me, *I* could settle the strike! I didn't like to say anything at the manufacturers' meeting the other night, especially with all those *Daitchen* present (a reference to the older, more cultured German element, who together with certain Gentile firms, represented the top-notchers in the industry). A woman isn't supposed to know anything about business, or dare open her mouth. But I could tell them a thing or two. So the factories would work nine hours instead of ten. Nine hours a day, six days a week, is enough, if only a man wants to work."

"And the piece-workers—what about them?" Papa asked.

"A little increase wouldn't hurt there either. The boss has nothing to lose. You pay those who produce and not the schlemiels who fall asleep over their work or run every minute to the water-closet." She halted Papa's exclamation of impatience. "They'll have to raise the pressers and the folders. I've seen myself a man cannot raise a family on ten or eleven dollars a week. Give them a dollar raise, and they won't listen to those agitators and walking delegates."

"Am I at last allowed to get in a word?" asked Papa impatiently. Thank you! There you stand in judgment like another King Solomon. Raise wages, shorten hours! Figure your wages, mine, Abe's, Harry's. I'm not counting Ephie's; he's only a beginner. But what about the investment on our capital? Aren't we entitled to some return on our investment? Money that we made, slaving for years, night and day. You know that every dollar we could spare we put back into the business for machines or another factory. Now, when we could produce, they go on strike!"

"That's exactly what I am trying to figure out," Mama answered quietly. "With all our work, why don't we make more money? Something is wrong somewhere. We can't raise the price of our shirts, our competitors would under-sell us. But you know who are our worst enemies? Fair competition one can meet. But those contractors who get shirts made in the tenements, the sweatshops—they are our real enemies, and the enemies of the working man, too. Who can compete with them? If I could figure how to save on the cloth, maybe use only a few inches less on every shirt—"

Mama picked up her sewing. "Tell me, Simon, does it say anything about the strike in the newspapers?"

"Nothing new, except that more and more are going back to work, just as I expected."

"Who was down today?"

"The same handful. Today it was Abraham and Sam Isaacs who nearly had their heads broken. I don't know what they want of us. Have I ever refused a man work, no matter how green he was? And I kept them, too, when the season was slack. Some are *frum* (pious), but you know as well as I, some are not. It isn't enough for them that the shop is closed on *Shabbus*, but just try to keep them a minute after half past three on Friday! You'd think they were *rovs* or *zaddicks* (rabbis or saints)! Our profit is reckoned in pennies on every shirt, and they expect me to perform miracles."

I listened hard to every word. It wasn't only that I had been watching Mama these last weeks as she waited for Papa and the boys to come home, night after night, and whispered, "Thank God, they're home safe." No, it wasn't that alone that made me want to cry out and tell Mama, that I was to Amy's house the other night. Her married sister was there, her husband worked in one of the shops that are on strike. They were suffering. She said that she had begged her husband to go back to his job, but he had refused to go and be a scab. When Amy's mother told her sister my name, she spat in my face and left the house. Amy cried and I cried.

"What's a scab, Amy?" I asked.

Amy didn't know either, but her mother said, "You know, my child, it is not good when working people do not stand together. If things in the trade are so bad that workers bring themselves to strike, how shameful it is for another worker to take his place. Such is a scab, my child. We do not blame your Mama and Papa—they alone cannot change anything."

Now, as I was listening to Papa and Mama I felt I had to speak out. "Mama," I began, but the words stuck in my throat. I was afraid of Papa's temper. I could just imagine what he would say: "You, an eleven-year-old nobody, who knows only how to waste her time learning to recite pieces and go to dancing school, you're going to give me advice on labor troubles!"

Mama's voice brought me back to reality. "Look,

there you sit dreaming, with your mouth wide open as if you were making speeches to yourself. Go to bed."

On Saturday night Uncle Israel came to see us. He, too, felt the need to talk things over. He sat next to my brother Harry, whom he loved very much. "He'll be the future head of the business one day," he once told Mama, at which she made believe she was very angry.

Uncle was talking in his soft, quiet manner, and everyone listened respectfully. "It's no use. The industry cannot afford to raise wages, not at the price they get for their merchandise. As for the closed shop, and to allow them to form a union, that is absolutely out of the question."

"But, Uncle," I piped up before I realized what I was saying, "if people who own factories can have an association, why can't those who work in them have one, too?"

Papa glared at me, too surprised to say anything. Mama gave me one of her "looks," but she said, without raising her voice, "Does she know what she's talking about? She was sitting in someone's house and they filled her ears with a lot of nonsense."

Uncle shook his head solemnly and said, "Children should be seen, but not heard."

"I don't know why she's allowed to be here altogether," blustered Abe.

"Ssh-Ssh, the parlor is too lonely, and the children are sleeping in the other rooms," Mama quickly answered him.

Harry had hardly noticed my excursion into the realm of labor problems, so occupied was he with his own thoughts. "If we could step up production or reduce other costs, an increase in wages wouldn't be impossible," he said.

Mama beamed. "God bless my Harry. Those were my very thoughts. I told your father only the other day that if a shirt could be cut, not so full, so that—"

"Fannie," Papa interrupted, a little anxiously, I thought, "Israel is not interested in your ideas."

"How about some fruit, Mama," Abe suggested, as if to cover up any embarrassment caused by Papa's remark. Soon everyone was busy peeling oranges and apples with the pearl-handled knives. Business was now put aside, and Mama made inquiries into the health and condition of my aunt and the children.

When Uncle finally left, Papa said, "You know, Fannie, for a smart woman you talk too much. The Proverbs say, 'He who speaks much, speaks foolishness.' Now what was the wonderful idea you were bursting to tell the world? Couldn't it wait until we are alone?"

"I was about to say that if instead of making a shirt like a nightgown, as large as a balloon, it was cut instead to fit closer to the body, we could save maybe five or six inches of material on every shirt. Can you imagine how much goods you would save on a hundred thousand dozen?"

Abe smiled appreciatively and Harry said, "That's a wonderful idea! You'll not only save yardage, but we'll have a better shirt."

Papa alone looked unconvinced. "It took me twenty years to perfect our patterns and train the cutters to satisfy our customers. Now I'll have to start all over again."

"It won't take twenty years to make this change," said Harry with finality.

A week later the strike was over. The workers went back, their strike lost. Nobody rejoiced. Perhaps both workers and bosses knew it was just a truce, that the battle was sure to be resumed.

Mama kept her promise, and wages were raised. "I cannot work with people and know that they are cursing me behind my back."

The faithful were, of course, rewarded first, but the increase trickled down to the steam pressers, the folders, the swatch-makers, all down the line. The ladies' underwear department was closed, and the girls all re-settled.

Mama kept up her weekly trips to the factory and always brought home a new set of patterns. At night she would sit comparing the old patterns with the new ones. She was certain that finally there would emerge a design which would save those inches of cloth. Then the new wage increase would not only be absorbed, but as she optimistically pointed out to Papa, it would enable them to triumph over their competitors.

✳

The Knipple

I knew little, if anything, about the value of money. There were no stores where we lived. When my mother ran short of some household item, there was nowhere she could send me to fetch it. There were no candy stores or toy shops.

But I did find coins useful. It was only in the wintertime, when Jack Frost came to visit us. He came early and remained long. When he first made his appearance in October or November, I was enchanted by the artistic designs painted on the windows. First a tracery of ferns and feathers and graceful swirls was etched. Gradually a fine lace curtain was drawn, though I could still see through it. But as the days went by, the lace turned into thick white snow, and I could not wipe it or scrape it away. For weeks and months the outdoors was shut out. It was too cold for me to venture forth, and I was only able to see the outside world through a peephole which I made by pressing a coin on the frosted pane. I depended on this small window—the larger the coin, the better would be my view of the vast world of snow. I believe the largest coin I used must have been a quarter; I don't remember any as large as a silver dollar, for there were no such denominations lying about.

From *Dakota Diaspora: Memoirs of a Jewish Homesteader,* by Sophie Trupin. University of Nebraska Press, 1988. © Copyright Sophie Trupin 1984. Reprinted with permission.

One day I learned that money had another use, equally important, and that the lack of it could create problems and strife. When my father came back from town he always brought my mother a tablet of white lined paper. She wrote regularly to my grandmother and often to her friends in the Old Country. I remember awakening at night to see her writing at the table, the kerosene lamp illuminating the white page. She would dip the pen in the inkwell, writing from right to left, which is the way Yiddish is written. She wrote the return address in English, which she practiced over and over again.

One day the tablet of paper had been used up and it was time to write a letter to my grandmother. My mother and I searched the entire house but we couldn't find a piece of paper that could serve the purpose. There is a saying in Yiddish, *"A guter yid git zich an aitzeh!"* Liberal translation: "A good Jew finds a way!" My mother found a way. She spied a tomato can with a garish red label. Carefully removing the paper, she used the reverse side to write her letter.

After my mother addressed the envelope, she found a new obstacle. She had used up all the stamps and also the money laid aside for that purpose. She asked my father for some money. I don't know whether he too was short of ready cash, but he did raise some objection. What had she done with the money he had given her? My mother was indignant. Was he counting every penny; were we that poor?

I believe it was from that day on that my mother, who had little experience with using money (since all the purchasing was done by my father or through mail order), started the practice of having a *knipple*. Every Jewish woman knows what that is; it's pin money that the husband knows nothing about, to be used only in the most dire emergencies. Many a husband, when in a tight spot financially, has been grateful to his wife for having kept aside some money for the *knipple*.

"Let God Worry A Little Bit"

"Money," my father used to say, "is of no consequence unless you owe it."

It was a point of honor with him to pay all debts when due. But, beyond that, Jake Edelstein was most casual about money. If an investment collapsed, as it frequently did, he'd say to mother, "Dinah, it was money we never had." When a real pinch came, and our household fund had to be commandeered for a creditor, Father would feel slightly sheepish. "Let God worry about us a little bit," he would say. Then he'd be off on his next business venture.

Over the years God must have worried a good deal. And the year I was 15 I shared His concern.

For several summers, Father had run Fleischmann's Hotel in the Catskill Mountains, near the village of Griffins Corners. It was a shoestring operation. Each season he opened by the grace of the local butcher, baker and hardware merchant; each Labor Day he paid off his debts. Then, consigning our worries to God, he would take us back to our New York flat and would work through the winter, managing a restaurant and saving toward another summer.

We loved the hotel; when, that spring, Father revealed that he just didn't have enough money to open

From *Molly and Me* by Gertrude Berg, 1961. Reprinted with permission for this edition from Aeonian Press, Inc., Mattituck, N.Y.

it, I was crushed. But, being 15 and sure of myself, I decided to take matters into my own hands. I went secretly to my grandfather.

Mordecai Edelstein had come to America as an immigrant tinsmith with a talent for hard work. After a lifetime of labor, he had retired from his sheet-metal business in New Jersey, a well-to-do and respected citizen. But the pride and independence that had made him what he was were matched in his son Jake, and as a result the two of them didn't get on well. The last man in the world Jake would have approached for a loan was his father.

"Grandfather," I said, "I've worked hard at the hotel every summer, and I think I should be a partner. Would you lend me the money to buy a partnership from Papa?"

Mordecai pulled at his white handlebar mustache. He understood the maneuver at once, and he knew that his son was ignorant of it. "So how much do you need?" he asked.

"Five thousand dollars."

"All right, but"—and he shook a bony finger under my nose—"remember *you're* the partner, not me."

When I presented the proposition to Father, he realized that my $5000 could have come only from Grandfather. But, so long as I didn't tell him, he could accept it, and that summer I endured for the first time the burden of debt. Every time a guest checked in, my heart was full of hope; every time one checked out I was in despair. All I could think of was the money I owed.

We had learned from experience that August 21 was the day when the hotel would begin to go into the black—if it was to go at all. The number of guests we retained from then until Labor Day made the summer worth-while or a failure, and from this day forward rain and boredom were our mortal enemies. They could empty the hotel like a plague.

On August 21 I awoke at dawn to hear horrible splashing on the roof. I ran to Father's room and cried out in a choking whisper, "It's raining!" Father nodded grimly and headed toward the kitchen.

"Everybody look pleasant!" he commanded the assembled waiters and bus boys. A glazed smile was set on each countenance as it went out to face the breakfast guests. But the guests failed to respond. It was raining, and they took it as a personal affront from the management.

After breakfast they all filed out to the veranda to sit in the rocking chairs and look at the sky. It remained gray and wet. Luncheon was more dolorous than breakfast. After lunch they returned to the rockers and the rain. The last train for New York left at four o'clock, and I knew that the moment the first woman announced her departure the exodus would begin.

I also knew who would be first to make the move—a Mrs. Goldenson, whose boredom threshold was low. I kept my eyes on her. What I would do I wasn't sure. I couldn't tie her to the rocker, but something heroic would be demanded.

At 3:15, exactly time to pack and get to the station, Mrs. Goldenson sighed and stood up.

"Mrs. Goldenson!" I almost screamed from the far end of the porch. "How would you like your palm read, your fortune told?"

I was aghast to hear those words coming out of my mouth. I didn't know the first thing about palmistry.

Mrs. Goldenson hesitated. "Fortunes you tell?"

I whipped out a large handkerchief and tied it around my head. I bent over like an old woman and put a crack in my voice. "We gypsies know the future," I cackled.

Mrs. Goldenson smiled and winked at the others, but she sat down and extended her hand. The others crowded around. For a moment I studied her palm, and suddenly I *did* see her future.

All that summer, from my favorite reading spot—a big lobby chair by a window that opened on the porch—I had overheard the gossip and confidences exchanged by the ladies while they rocked. I had stored up everything I heard, and now it was my salvation.

Bending over Mrs. Goldenson's hand, I murmured, "You are a fortunate woman. You have the love of two men."

"Ah?" breathed the circle of kibitzers, pressing closer.

"One is rather short, middle-aged. I think he is bald. . . ."

"Herman," she said with pleased possessiveness.

"The other is young and tall and handsome."

"Stanley, my son," she announced to the ladies.

"I see the two of them close together . . . I think in an office. . . ."

"Supreme Fashions," she said.

"I see a cloud coming between you and your son Stanley."

"Never! What kind of a cloud?"

"It's not clear. Perhaps . . . another woman. Yes, a woman. She's in the same office with your husband and son."

"Eunice Meyers!" cried Mrs. Goldenson, striking her forehead with the palm of the hand I was trying to read. "I told Herman not to hire that girl!"

"I see a wedding," I said.

"I'll die!" she wailed. Then she stood up and said, "I have to telephone New York."

A few minutes later she returned to the porch. "Miss Edelstein, please make another room available. My husband and my son Stanley will be coming up this week-end."

Grandfather's money was safe for another 24 hours! The following morning the blessed sun shone.

Day by day I watched the ledger figures creep toward the black until our sole debt was the one that weighed most heavily upon me: Grandfather's loan. What if it rained again? I couldn't count on fortune-telling a second time. Then came another inspiration.

At dinner one evening I announced the production of a children's play, with auditions the next morning. I sat up that night to write the play—a mixture of Cinderella, Robin Hood, and Little Women. My problem was one not of art but of numbers. Our guests were 50-percent women, 40-percent children and 10-percent week-end commuting husbands. I hoped to tie down as many children as possible.

The auditions were successful beyond my wildest hopes. Every child in the hotel appeared, some voluntarily, some prodded—and suddenly I had a cast of 35. Rehearsals were started, and after a week the parents began to demand a performance. I explained that more rehearsals would be necessary. A Mrs. Lowen wasn't satisfied. "Why can't we have the play tomorrow?" she asked.

"The actors aren't ready," I explained. "We need at least another week."

"I'm not expecting to stay so long. Maybe I'll have to take Patty out of the play."

Mrs. Lowen made a wry face. Patty was a spoiled brat, and we both knew that she'd scream bloody murder if Mrs. Lowen attempted such a thing.

At last I set the date for the performance: Labor Day, the last day of the hotel season. And I suggested that it would be nice for the cast to invite their uncles and aunts and cousins to come for the week-end.

I think the play went off reasonably well. After the performance, however, I came face to face with Mrs. Lowen. "Ten days I stayed over so Patty could be an actress," she said. "And what does Patty have to say? One speech, six words—I counted them. That's less than a word a day!"

"Patty had to serve an apprenticeship," I said. "Next year she'll have one of the leads."

"Yoweeee!" Patty exulted.

The morning after Labor Day, Father and I sat together in the tiny office while I ran up the figures on the adding machine. My hand trembled slightly as the total mounted. The final figure was $5367.92.

"We made it!" I cried.

I felt wonderfully free, and when Father pointed out that we would be practically broke after I had added interest to the loan, I said happily, "Let God worry about us a little bit."

Father laughed and threw his arms around me.

❋

Four Homes in One Year

We lived in four homes that first year.

We lasted one month in the rooms my father had prepared for us on Ninth Street and Avenue C. That place was unacceptable, even by our diminished standards. The toilets were privies in the cellar, two flights down dimly lit stairs. That was for the Hottentots, my mother declared. "I will look for something better."

My mother was an energetic lady. She began talking to people she met in stores. The grocery store was her most productive source of information; but any information that might possibly lead to another apartment was collected. In the end it was the grocery-store lady who led my mother to our next home.

Incidentally, when we first arrived in New York, and, for quite a few years after, I cannot recall the use of the word "apartment," or even "flat," when people referred to their living quarters. It was always the "place," or the "rooms"—never the "apartment."

But before we left that Ninth-Street place, we had our first experience with the rugged July Fourth celebrations of that time. And a hair-raising experience it was. Someone had told Papa that on that one day, Indians with firearms were brought into the city and given

From *A Time To Remember: Growing Up in NY Before the Great War*, by Marie Jastrow. NY: W.W. Norton & Co. 1979. © Reprinted with permission of Robert Jastrow.

free reign to fill the street with their shooting and savagery. We spent that first July Fourth huddled together in our rooms, trying to understand the fearful din going on outside. I remember my mother hanging a heavy quilt across the window that faced the street, and how frightened we were. Those wild, lusty July Fourths were enough to terrify any European. And Mama was not too certain whether America was for her after all; she was ready to go back home "where civilized people lived."

On the first of August we moved to Seventy-sixth Street and Second Avenue. That apartment wasn't much better, but the toilet was upstairs, a few feet from our door. We shared it with another family who lived across the hall. It was not the best of arrangements, but better than going down those dark cellar steps.

The facilities for taking a bath seemed odd indeed—two washtubs, with a removable center partition. We tried to accept the convertible washtubs as part of the American scene, but bathing became a chore, no fun for anyone—unless he was acrobatically inclined—to climb into the makeshift tub. At first we were amused. If this was the way Americans bathed, who were we to argue.

Later, we learned that many bathtubs in New York City were in bathrooms, and many toilets were private.

By the time we found that out, it was too late; Papa hated moving; and besides, the rent was cheap. When my mother broached the subject, Papa dodged the issue in his usual way; he went back to his reading. The subject was closed.

My mother knew, however, that sooner or later Papa would get sick of the makeshift bathtub. At the end of the summer, she went about finding another flat again, this time with a private bathroom. As usual, the grocery store was her source of information. Yes, there was a very fine place on 92nd Street, boasting its own bathroom. Mama rented the rooms. That evening, realizing she had walked rashly into a situation that would become more difficult with every moment of delay, she went directly to the point. "I have found a place with a private bathroom."

My father laid down his book. "Really? Where?" Suddenly he took in the full meaning of my mother's words.

"You didn't—"My mother shook her head, "I did." "But hear what I have to say before you get angry. There is a bathroom opening onto a hall. But the hall is in the flat. Our personal private hall and bathroom."

The private bathroom was a point that my father could not argue. Then he remembered the moving expenses from Seventy-sixth Street to Ninety-second Street. For this financial problem my mother came up with a happy solution. She had learned of it by accident. It was simply that people who moved withheld the last month's rent to cover the moving expenses. It was done all the time in America. It was the custom. People said that if moving became a necessity, the fault lay with the landlord. Who else? So, let him pay. It was a custom my mother agreed with heartily. America had some fine customs.

My father threw up his hands. What can one do with such a woman?

We moved one month later, on the first of October.

The landlord sighed, and rented the rooms to other tenants. There were no leases those days. At least, not where we lived.

It was a nice enough flat on Ninety-second Street. The kitchen was exceptionally large. My mother liked moving about in large kitchens.

The apartment was located in the rear of the building. All the windows looked down into the courtyard. Most of the winter the yard was covered with snow. But when the snow melted and the warm days of May came, from the yard below rose smells that made it seem as if all the eggs of the world were rotting there. We kept our windows closed whenever possible, but in the heat of summer, when all the windows would be open, what then? Disaster stared us in the face. Mama was ready to move again.

This time the grocery store was no help. My mother was desperate—that awful smell. My father agreed ruefully that other quarters must be found, although he recoiled at the thought of moving again. He had become used to Ninety-second Street. He knew when the elevated train came by, and how long it took him to get to his job; he stopped to chat every evening with the newspaper man who had his stand at the foot of the stairs to the El; and he liked the warm greetings from people in the train who went to work and came home the same time with him every day.

Well, on the first of June, we moved again.

This time, it was my father who found our new home. He had learned of a modern, steam-heated tenement on Eighty-first Street near the East River.

My mother was never one to let grass grow under her feet. The next morning she asked a neighbor, "Is it too far to walk to Eighty-first?" adding, "It is near the river."

No, they were only short blocks, not far at all. My mother took me firmly by the hand and we walked to Eighty-first Street to inspect the rooms in that modern, steam-heated building. Mama was enchanted by what she saw! A white porcelain sink, hot water, a gas stove, and a white bathtub! The vacant rooms were on the third floor. One room faced the street. It was nice to have a room facing the street, Mama said. There were two bedrooms, a kitchen and the "front room." The janitor said the landlord lived in the building.

Mama gave a deposit.

In the evening my father listened to my mother recite the wonders of that marvelous flat. "Imagine, a gas stove for the cooking," Mama was really excited. "When I think of all the ashes I sifted for the coal that didn't burn, my God! No more ashes to get into everything, a stove that bakes and cooks when you strike a match, I can't believe it."

My father cleared his throat, but no one paid attention. "And there is the bedroom off the hall, a personal private hall, separate; I mean, this room is separate from the rest of the place," she explained.

"That's nice," my father said. "Buy why do we need one room separated from the rest of the family?"

"For the boarder."

"The boarder? What boarder?" My father's voice became shrill, "You didn't rent—you didn't—not with a boarder."

"No, of course not. Where would I get a boarder in such a hurry? I paid a deposit," she added quickly.

My father was stunned. Such fast action was too much for him. He liked to mull things over. But Mama never turned things over in her mind longer than it took her to decide one way or another. Especially when such marvelous things as white sinks, gas stoves and separate rooms for boarders were in jeopardy.

Papa recovered his voice. "How much is the rent?"

My mother squared her shoulders. "Nine dollars."

"Nine dollars." My father's face was getting redder and redder. "My God, do you know what you have done? Nine dollars for rent—I only make eight dollars a week."

"Don't worry—we will manage. It's such a beautiful place. You will be happy there. Some day you will thank me," she added.

"But that high rent—we only pay seven here."

Two dollars was the difference between eating well and not eating well. A loaf of bread was four cents; a quart of rich, good milk was four cents; a dozen eggs cost ten cents.

Mama revealed her plan.

"We will take a boarder. He will help with the rent."

"No! No boarder!" My father's voice was final. He went back to his paper.

My mother said nothing. When Papa came home on the last day of the month, he found an empty apartment and a note telling him to come to Eighty-first Street. We had packed and moved into that modern tenement with its steam heat, hot water and white porcelain sink. Mama had decided to face him with the accomplished fact. And it worked. Everything went along splendidly. My father rang the bell, stepped into his new home as if nothing had happened, washed his hands, and sat down to eat.

It was the fuss and disorder of packing and moving that he hated, and my mother knew that. Later, my father admitted that Mama had been right.

Perhaps I should add that eventually Mama overcame my father's objections to a boarder and rented the hall bed room for two dollars a week. I was transferred to a makeshift bed in the front room.

My Story

*A first-person account by Rachel Bella Calof of the early
years of homesteading in North Dakota, 1894 to 1910.
Rachel, born in 1876, in Russia, was four years old when
her mother died, leaving Rachel, an older brother, a young
sister and a baby brother of 18 months. The family had
a difficult life, especially after her father remarried, and
separated the children who lived in two different towns.
Later when Rachel was 18, her uncle arranged for her to
substitute for another as a possible mate for a young man
who had immigrated to the US. After an exchange of pho-
tos, Rachel is interviewed by Chaya, the intermediary ar-
ranging the betrothal.*

Chaya now decided to examine me in greater detail.
She said she wanted to know me better, and to visit her
for the next Sabbath. I didn't have a proper dress for
such an invitation, but I was anxious to make good, and
was finally able to borrow a dress for the occasion. I
spent three days under close observation and undergo-
ing various kinds of testing. As an example, I was

From the unpublished ms of the above name, © 1936 by Rachel
Bella Calof. Tr. from the Yiddish by Jacob Calof and Molly Shaw.
Reprinted by permission of Jacob Calof. (not for further use)

handed a ball of tangled yarn to unravel. I didn't understand the purpose for this, but I succeeded in unraveling all the yarn. My future sister-in-law was quite pleased. She explained that this was a way of testing my patience and good nature. She said that had I become angry or frustrated in attempting to unravel the thread, I would have lost the opportunity of marrying the boy in America. Thank God I passed all the tests. God was watching over me and I won Chaya's approval.

*   *   *

Rachel is met at Ellis Island in the USA by Abraham, who takes her to his boarding house in New York City. She sleeps in the dining room cupboard and Abraham stays on a couch nearby. The place is infested with cockroaches, and the arrangements make her apprehensive. She observes that Abraham has spoken to the landlord and his wife to improve their condition:

Even though everything and everyone seemed so strange, including my boyfriend, I felt that the boy was more of a friend to me than any of the other people I had met. I thought about this for some time and decided that probably my future still lay with him. So I rededicated myself to our common cause, and by the time Abraham returned from his work I was indeed glad to see him.

After supper he suggested that we go for a walk. I instinctively resisted this proposal. Although I was determined to try to build a future with Abraham, I meant to do so only if I could be assured that he proved to be a man of acceptable character. As of the moment, I was not prepared to trust him fully. Although my great uncle had spoken favorably about the boy, he had already been in America three years, and I suspected that a person's character could change considerably in less time than that in America. Well, I decided to do my share in developing trust between us and so I consented to go for a walk in New York with an almost stranger. Maybe I was changing too.

*   *   *

Rachel is now on the land homesteaded by Abraham's family near Devil's Lake, North Dakota. It is her second day after her arrival. Six adults and one child sleep in a wooden shack 12 ft. by 14 ft. Rachel is obliged to share her bed with the grandmother and the child, who relieves himself during the night. She is shocked at the primitive and hard life facing her, mindful of her 19 years of hardship:

I began the following morning by protesting that I could not again sleep with the child. The grandmother answered briefly and decisively. This was the way it must be, and the sleeping arrangement would continue. I understood then I was not to speak of this again, but I knew I was stronger for having expressed myself and would better face up to the tests which I knew were ahead.

The very next day brought a new blow. The men held a meeting to make plans for getting through the winter. They decided that Abraham was to work three months at the homestead of the one settler in the area who was not a Calof. His place was five miles or so distant. He was better off than most, and had been offered $75. for three months work on his homestead, which was already under cultivation. This money could provide the necessities which would enable three Calof families to survive the winter. I raised my voice against the arbitrary selection of Abraham. Why not one of the other two brothers, I demanded to know? The answer was swift and certain. Women, I was informed, had no judgment or voice in matters of importance. Unmistakably the subject was closed, but at least all concerned had learned that I had a voice and the will to use it where my welfare was concerned.

I accompanied Abraham to his place of work, and after a few parting words, began my return. That walk back across the lonely prarie proved to be a momentous testing for me. A veritable torrent of emotions flowed through my mind. Except for Abraham's return for a few hours on weekends, I would be alone in the terrible new world in which I now lived, and I would have to fight my battle without my only ally. Looking across the great plain, I knew a loneliness which seared my very soul. Who belongs to me, and to whom do I belong, I questioned? I was young and healthy and had always had a zest for life despite my meager past. Still these qualities seemed inadequate to lead me out of the nightmare existence I had fallen into. I sat on a stone in the high grass and gave myself up to utter despair.

So great was my anguish that sense of time and place faded from my consciousness. There remained only a void of misery, and I prayed with a terrible intensity to God to show me mercy and the way to a better life.

After a time, the storm of my emotions passed and I arose from the ground. My mind was clear and calm. The resentment and rebellion born in the last two days had solidified into a new strength which was to serve me well from that time forward.

* * *

Soon after, Rachel resolves not to surrender to the harsh conditions of living on the plains, and comes up with at least one solution:

As night approached, I told the old lady that I was not content to go to bed at sundown. I informed her that I would try to bring light into the shack. I went outside to see what materials nature might provide for my project, and soon found some partly dried mud, which I moulded into a narrow container. I shaped a wick out of a scrap of rag, smeared it with butter, placed it in the mud cup, and lit it and lo and behold, there was light. Everyone was delighted with my invention. Now we could retire at a more reasonable hour. Now we were able to undress and prepare for bed in a civilized way. This accomplishment stands out in my mind as the first result of my effort to climb out of the mire which surrounded me.

The wedding of Rachel and Abraham has already been performed in sincere style, with other Jewish men and women coming from the area and title taken for their acres of land from the US government, but the families are still living in very crowded and painful conditions, especially the women. (The men hire themselves out to nearby farmers to earn money) Rachel finds her domestic efforts thwarted:

I put forth my best efforts to maintain some level of cleanliness in this hellish environment, but as yet can well imagine, it was a battle doomed to failure. In retrospect I can understand the strain that Abe was under in the multiple roles he played in the small society of that shack. He was father, husband, son and brother to us and he was the target of everyone's complaints and suggestions. I was an intolerable load, and he finally sought relief by striking out at probably the only one there who was capable of receiving criticism. One day, like a bolt from the blue, he announced that he would have to divorce me because of the dirty condition of my house. Of course, I know now that his action was a result of the stress under which we all lived, but when it happened I was in no mood to spend any time in analyzing the underlying reasons for his accusation. I was outraged at his charge and defended myself vigorously. I couldn't understand why he refused to recognize the impossible conditions which confronted me, and I stood face to face with him and gave as good as I received. I remembered his words with bitterness and tears for a long time to come. I had suffered many privations in my determination to stand shoulder to shoulder with him, from Russia to this miserable shack, conducting myself under the most severe conditions as a Jewish woman should, and now to be threatened by divorce on the grounds of being dirty was to me the greatest degradation. Many events may have faded from memory, but this insult remained.

❋

Sisters

At fourteen, Sheyna* was a revolutionary, an earnest, dedicated member of the Socialist-Zionist movement, and as such doubly dangerous in the eyes of police and liable to punishment. Not only were she and her friends "conspiring" to overthrow the all-powerful czar, but they also proclaimed their dream to bring into existence a Jewish socialist state in Palestine. In the Russia of the early twentieth century, even a fourteen- or fifteen year-old schoolgirl who held such views would be arrested for subversive activity, and I still remember hearing the screams of young men and women being brutally beaten in the police station around the corner from where we lived.

My mother heard those screams, too, and daily begged Sheyna to have nothing to do with the movement; she could endanger herself and us and even Father in America! But Sheyna was very stubborn. It was not enough for her to want changes; she had to participate in bringing them about. Night after night, my mother kept herself awake until Sheyna came home from her mysterious meetings, while I lay in bed, taking it all in silently: Sheyna's devotion to the cause in which she believed so strongly; Mother's overwhelming anxi-

---

*Sheyna was the older sister of Golda Meier, who became Prime Minister of Israel, 1969–74.

From *My Life* by Golda Meier. © NY: The Putnam Publishing Group, 1975. Reprinted with permission.

ety; Father's (to me, inexplicable) absence; and the periodic and fearful sound of hooves of Cossack horses outside.

Although the yearning of the Jews for their own land was not the direct result of pogroms (the idea of the Jewish resettlement of Palestine had been urged by Jews and even some non-Jews long before the word "pogrom" became part of the vocabulary of European Jewry), the Russian pogroms of my childhood gave the idea immediacy, especially when it became clear to the Jews that the Russian government itself was using them as scapegoats of the regime's struggle to put down the revolutionary movement. . . .

On Saturdays, when Mother went off to the synagogue, Sheyna organized meetings at home. Even when Mother found out about them and pleaded with Sheyna not to imperil us, there was nothing she could do about these meetings except nervously walk up and down outside the house when she got back on Saturday morning, patrolling it like a sentry so that when a policeman approached, she could at least warn the young conspirators.

Sometimes, when Sheyna and I got into a fight and I lost my temper, I used to threaten to tell Maxim, the big, red-faced policeman in our neighborhood, all about her political activities. Of course, I never did, and of course, Sheyna knew that my threats were empty; but they worried her all the same. "What will you tell Maxim?" she asked. "I'll tell him that you and all your friends want to do away with the czar," I would shriek.

"Do you know what will happen to me then? I'll be sent away to Siberia, where I'll die of cold and never come back," she'd say. "That's what happens to people who are exiled."

Truth to tell, I was always very careful to keep out of Maxim's way. Whenever I saw him lumbering in my direction, I took to my heels and fled. . . .

❋

Glimpses of Grandmothers

About Ida Richter:

There were all kinds of [political] parties. There was the Zion-Labor parties, the Socialist Democratic Party, the Bund, the Socialist Party, the Anarchist Party.

My father had a man working for him, a young man, Jewish. Somebody snitched on him that he's a leader in the youth. So the *zhandarm* came to look for this man and his name was Yankel. "Where's Yankel?" My mother knew. A night before, she dressed him up in women's clothes, and he laid on a roof in an attic across the street. But my mother had made some bread for the week, and she put it on the couch and covered it up with a tablecloth; and the police thought that the man was there. They went and grabbed it, so my mother thought: "He's going to take it away! We'll have no bread for the week." So she went before him to cover [it] with her body, like you can't take it. Well, he threw her across the floor and uncovered that, and the boy wasn't there. Anyhow, they took him in a covered wagon to the next city and put him on the train to Germany, and he waited for the ship to come to America. A Jew

From *Jewish Grandmothers* by Sydelle Kramer and Jenny Masur. Copyright © 1976 by Beacon Press. Reprinted with permission. See also note, p. 115.

would help a Jew in anything because, if not, then who would help him?

About Mollie Linker:

I was always a fighter. My grandchildren call me the Communist, the rebel. Naturally, we were third class [on the boat], you know. What did they give us to eat? Well, most of them were strictly Orthodox so they couldn't eat meat anyway, so they gave us herring and potatoes. But I always wanted to see a lot. I came up on the deck—I always used to be on the deck to see fish and the ocean. That's how I met the captain; and I must have sneaked down one day in the first class or second, I saw children were given fruit or candy; and I came up and spoke to the captain. I was not afraid. Probably I spoke in Russian because we spoke Russian more than Jewish. And I said to him, "How come there are so many children down here and they don't get fruit or candy?" The next day, there was a big basket of fruit and candy for the children. That was my first fight.

* * *

At fifteen, I took almost three hundred people on strike. Must have been [there] about six months. The building was an old tall building and there were only two small elevators. So whoever got in, got in, and the rest couldn't get in. [Then] one wasn't working and they didn't bother to fix it. You had to wait a long [time] or walk to the fifth floor, or they'd be late to work. You wanted to make your money; you were working piece-work. Some people couldn't walk up that high.

And one day, it dawned on me—why should these older people, old men and women, walk up to the fifth floor? I stood up a couple of times; I says, "Let's go to the union." The foreman wasn't around—you'd get fired. I think they must have been flabbergasted that a young girl can do things like that 'cause there was no comment—we just went. We marched all the way to the union. That day we stayed out of work; there was no picketing. The next day, the elevator was fixed; and then we used the elevators. That's why my grandchildren call me Red. I was always doing those things.

* * *

About Sarah Rothman, the watchmaker:

After the first year, I wanted to get a divorce because I was going through an awful lot, you know; the whole family was on my shoulders. Especially in a small town, and he [my husband] is the big shot from that town, everybody knows who is his wife and who is his father-in-law and who is his mother-in-law. The police station was across the street of my house.

So I said, "Look. You promised me not to participate anymore, not to be that active, you understand." He was very busy. The Bolsheviks made him a big shot. I wanted him to stop. I used to be so tired, and he used to come so late, two, three o'clock in the morning, and not having a key. He used to knock on my window to open the door for him; and I accepted the waking up the family, my father and my mother, so he could go to his meetings. [But finally] I gave him an ultimatum.

I couldn't sacrifice my family. Many times I was thinking of my personal life, my children. I says, "You should choose—either the Party or me." He says, "No. I love you too much to give you up! I wouldn't do it." See over there, for five rubles, you got a divorce from the rabbi. He wouldn't want to give me a divorce.

[But he went anyway to fight] with the Bolsheviks. There was civil war and fighting. Then the bands came, and he heard that we had a *pogrom* in our town. He don't know if I'm alive, if the baby is alive. Denikin or Kolchak or Balachowicz was in our town and they killed a lot of people. The peasants said, "Balachowicz is here; you cannot save yourself."

We escaped. I had a Jewish couple that lived with me, and he had a horse and wagon. And he took me with the baby, with my sister, to hide ourselves at the peasants' in the little villages, I never thought that I'm gonna be alive. My father-in-law was killed: he went to *shul* to pray. A priest hid my mother-in-law. A woman was sitting milking a cow—they came and killed her.

I took all the watches with me. I knew they were going to rob everything in the house. They took even out the windows. When we came back, we found only four walls. The doors they took out. The peasants helped them; they said the Jews were Bolsheviks.

I took the Gentiles watches—that saved us; otherwise, they wouldn't take us in. They were nice but they were afraid for their own lives. Some were afraid the others shouldn't tell that they're hiding Jews in the house. "I'll let you sleep here but the next day, you should leave my house because I'm afraid the others would tell." [They fed us] baked potatoes, tea with saccharin. Then we went further down and further down; we knew the bandits wouldn't be long in power—the Bolsheviks would come back. A couple of weeks we ran, [each night] in different places.

[When my husband came back], he was captured by the bands. The main officer of the post office, a Gentile, I used to fix watches for him, I didn't charge him. Once, they thought that he's against the Bolsheviks, so they arrested him. So I went, and I said, "This man you're taking, this man who had five children and a family, he didn't do anything wrong." And they let him go.

So when they arrested my husband, right away he heard—it's a small town. He came and he says, "[I came] as soon as I saw in the papers what's going on, that your husband is arrested. You don't have to be afraid. I happen to be a friend of the leader of the band. I'll go there and I'll talk to him." And he did. He went there with me, and everybody saw him going with me. They thought that he's going to tell on my husband, on me, but he remembered what I did for him when he was in trouble.

Note: The foregoing were rendered from oral histories; all names being pseudonyms. Sarah Rothman was one of the few women in Eastern Europe to practice a trade (watchmaking) in the early 1900's. Mollie Linker, at 74, a well-read woman, once owned a school bookstore and read all of the 750 titles sold; Ida Richter, once a dutiful daughter of the shtetl, became a successful business woman in the US, and wrote several novels.

✽

Fear: Berlin, *1938*

We three women, mother, daughter and cook, eyed the sinister-looking saber and stiletto with terror. They were my father's sidearm, left over from World War I and now obsolete.

I was bitter and angry at my older brother who had overlooked these weapons during a previous search of the loft for these weapons. This carelessness was a dangerous oversight, and if discovered by the Gestapo could have resulted in our father's arrest.

My mother's mind was flooded with terror and paralyzing fear for my father's safety. It blocked her capacity to act. Those ten dreadful days which had been filled with violent persecutions by jeering mobs, the sounds of shattering glass, sights of burning synagogues, invasions of privacy of Jewish homes and places of work, with men being dragged from their work even in the midst of performing operations, and searches for weapons, gold, jewelry, subversive literature and correspondence, left my mother completely stunned.

I said, "We must get rid of it immediately, there is no time to be lost, now that all legal ways are closed to turn the weapons in." To myself, I mused how strange it was how we still clung to legal ways, though the government did not seem to bother anymore. The weapons

From an unpublished memoir by Liselotte Bendix Stern. Reprinted by special permission for this edition.

had to be wrapped and the parcel had to be smuggled out of the house in the dark. We had decided to take it to a nearby forest preserve and drown it in the lake.

My mother was too agitated to come along with me, so I went to the living room to ask my brother-in-law for help. At that hour the whole family was usually gathered in the living room, reading peacefully. However tonight no one was there, except for my sister and her husband. My brother was in hiding, staying with American relatives while my father had gone to Leipzig to give comfort and advice to his besieged sister and brother-in-law. Edith and Ernst were sitting on the sofa in the warm glow of the reading lamp looking rather peaceful and unconcerned, completely absorbed in their own problems. I felt that this was quite inappropriate and it filled me with rage. Without mincing words, I told them of our lethal discovery and demanded that Ernst should accompany me to the nearby lake.

My sister blurted "You keep out of it, Ernst, you must not get involved in this affair. You are waiting for your passport and permit to leave for England. You must keep yourself safe." When she refused to finish washing the dinner dishes to relieve the cook who was determined to accompany me, I became even more furious. Her refusal to help was especially objectionable since these two had invited themselves for the customary Friday night dinner—though this was certainly not an ordinary Friday night and had caused extra work for the cook.

In the rear of the apartment the two older women were frantically searching for large sheets of unmarked wrapping paper and cardboard. On the back stairs, which were hardly ever used by anyone at night, heavy footsteps were heard stomping up and down. To us they sounded like the heavy booted footfalls of the feared Storm Troopers. Our panic increased. After what had seemed to have been an eternity, the adequate, anonymous wrappings were found, the weapons were wrapped into a hugh parcel, and disguised the best we could. Marie, the cook, and I hurriedly dressed, and my mother saw us off with a worried smile, her brown eyes glittering with suppressed tears.

We managed to slip out of the house unnoticed and walked rapidly along the dark streets. I kept at a fast clip which was hard on the elderly, chubby cook. We were both driven by fear, every footstep behind us seeming a threat. Marie, who had known me since babyhood, insisted on carrying the disguised weapons herself to protect us in case we might be stopped. Marie was in a state of hysterics due to the fear during the past few days that the secret police might turn and take the men of the family away to one of the dreaded concentration camps.

I loved our cook and sensed her state of mind, and in spite of my own uneasiness I distracted her by making plans for the future when we would all be safe in America.

The dark streets were quite deserted. Only the boarded-up shop windows of Jewish owned stores and the piles of shattered glass heaped at the curbs, bore witness to the mob scenes that had raged through the streets a few days ago.

We finally reached the forest which had been our family recreation spot. As I knew the neighborhood well, we quickly found our way to the nearest lake. We stood on the bridge hiding the ominous parcel under our arms as we leaned on the bridge in apparent quiet conversation, intent on admiring the reflection of the starry sky on the water, but scanning furtively for possibly dangerous passersby. As soon as we were sure we were alone we lifted our arms in perfect unison and let go of our burden. It hit the water with a loud splash. We feared it could be heard for miles away. To our relief, it was sinking rapidly to the bottom of the lake after bobbing up a few times. We walked away quickly still looking fearfully over our shoulders. We felt the villas around the lake had a million eyes, though all the windows were pitch dark.

Now that we had rid ourselves of our burden, Marie remembered she had neglected to go to the bathroom before we had left home, so now she was overcome by this very human need. Laughingly we stopped at a secluded spot and Marie disappeared into the bushes while I stood watch. The absurdity of this mundane occurrence in the midst of our worries provided a comic relief and left a deep impression on me.

When this second and minor crisis was over, we walked arm in arm to the next streetcar. With the treacherous parcel gone we felt we were no longer fugitives and could join humanity once again and come into the light. But we did interrupt our ride once to phone my mother, saying, "We haven given the baby its bath and will be home shortly." (Everyone spoke in coded phrases those days) My mother understood immediately; a sigh of relief was her answer.

Once home my mother opened the door instantly when she heard the stopping elevator. She brought out the best French brandy and all three of us sat around the table sipping the warm drink.

As so often during those dangerous weeks the roles had been reversed. It seemed to me that I had become the protective parent and that my parents depended on my judgment and courage. It seemed to make the thought of my impending departure for good even harder to bear.

�֎

Alicia

Encouraged by Manka's friendship and because I needed to earn food, I decided to visit an older couple whose farm was in a nearby Ukrainian village. I had worked for them several times during the summer and, although they might have guessed who I really was, they didn't seem to mind as long as I worked hard in their field. They told me that if I ever came to their village I should visit their house and they would give me food.

I was hesitating about going into a Ukrainian village, and thought about it all Saturday night. When I awoke to a bright Sunday morning, I decided to visit the farm. I had to time my arrival at the village so that most people would be in church and the roads would be empty.

Moving as quietly as possible so as not to disturb the sleeping people on the floor, I washed my face with cold water, combed and braided my hair, put on my blanket skirt, and wrapped rags around my feet before slipping them into my already too small wooden-soled shoes. Before leaving I picked up the small bundle I had made the night before—two roundish stones the size of eggs wrapped in a kerchief. They were part of the story I planned to tell anyone, if necessary; I was on my way to the village to see the Wrozka, a sort of witch-charmer, to seek help for my mother, who was about to have a baby and was not feeling too well. This story would go well with the superstitious Ukrainians, I knew. Almost every village had some kind of charmer who could cast favorable (or unfavorable) spells, predict the future, or provide charms for a price. My payment would be the make-believe eggs.

This particular village was to the east; I figured a good two hours' walk from Wujciu's, and I was in a hurry to get started. But before leaving the kitchen to go out, I stopped and turned to look at my mother. This had become a habit with me, for even considering the comparative safety of Wujciu's home, I could never be sure that I would see her again. I could be caught or they could be discovered. Indeed, I never left the house without feeling that I might be looking at my dear mother for the last time. Those partings always made me very unhappy; and I was just as glad my mother didn't wake up to see me go.

I wrapped Slavka's woolen scarf tightly around my head and over my nose and throat, put on the jacket, and left, closing the door quietly behind me.

It was a beautiful morning. For all the discomfort it brought, I really loved the snow. It made everything look so peaceful and fairy-tale-like, particularly when the sun was first coming out and the reflections made the ice crystals look like thousands of tiny glittering diamonds. Snow had fallen the previous night, but not enough to cover the sleigh marks on the roads connecting the villages. At this time of day, and especially because it was Sunday, the roads were deserted. As I walked I could hear sleighbells in the distance. People were traveling to church. Thus absorbed in the beauty of the morning and caught up in a kind of dreamlike state, I did not hear the approach of a sleigh until it was almost upon me. I moved over to let it pass. I was prepared to call out my greetings as the sleigh and its occupants passed me, but I choked on my words. There, leaving me behind but slowing down to have a better look at me, was a sleigh full of blue-uniformed men: Ukrainian police.

I felt as though I had been kicked in the stomach. I had to think quickly before they realized that I had no business being on this road on a Sunday morning dressed in rather shabby clothing; they might get suspicious and ask questions. I had to do something.

"Wait!" I cried. "Wait a minute, will you?" Waving both arms, I rushed forward to the sleigh, now slowing to a stop. "Can you give me a ride into the village ahead of us?" I asked while pulling my shawl over my face.

"I am on my way to see the Wrozka. My mother is in labor and having a hard time and my father sent me to get her blessing. Can you help?" I asked, almost crying. I must have sounded convincing to them, because one of them answered.

"You are in luck. I'm from the village, and I know just where she lives. Climb in; we will take you right to her door."

As arms reached out to help me into the sleigh, a shudder passed through my body. For a fleeting moment I saw the madness of my situation. They, thinking me a Ukrainian girl, treated me nicely. They pulled part of the blanket from their knees to my back. Then the fear set in. I remembered another ride on a sleigh, to the prison in Chortkov, and now I really shivered. Although I was able to control my body, I was trembling inside all the time.

It took about twenty minutes to get to the village. The policemen drove me through the village right to the door of a mud house. I thanked them profusely, keeping my head bowed, and one of them patted me on the back and offered words of encouragement about my mother's welfare. They were in a merry mood. I was hoping they would pull away at that point, but they remained to see that I got safely inside the house. So I had no other choice but to knock on the door.

The door was opened by an old woman with long gray hair. She was a homely old woman, missing all her teeth. She really looked like the picture of "wicked witches" in children's books. I must admit she scared me. I had never before seen one of these women, and looking at her now, it occurred to me that she might be able to see right through my lies and might immediately know who I was. Yet there I stood, clutching my little kerchief with the two round rocks, explaining my mother's supposed problem to her. She gave me one long, piercing look and invited me inside.

There was only one large open room, dark except for the glow of a fireplace. It was an eerie room, and the floor looked as though it had not been swept in quite some time. The woman asked me to sit on a chair by the fireplace, where a large kettle was suspended.

I felt strangely fascinated and curious as I was plunged into an atmosphere of sorcery and dark magic. The woman bustled about the room, her long, raggedy skirt sweeping up little clouds of unswept dust as she searched her shelves for certain herb jars.

"What is your name, my dear?" she asked.

"Slavka," I said timidly.

"And your mother's?"

"Maria." She nodded thoughtfully and spilled a number of different herbs onto the little workbench. She chopped them all together and carried the mixture over to the kettle, which was already steaming. Solemnly she threw the herbs into the bubbling liquid, causing it to give off a mighty hiss and a foul smell. She stirred the kettle with a long wooden spoon. Then, dipping a red rag into the pot, she sprinkled the brew first into the fire, mumbling something as she did so, and then

——— 123 ———

onto me. I wanted to run out of that crazy place, but I remembered the Ukrainian police who might still be outside, so I dropped back into the chair and tried not to breathe in the foul odor. She repeated the sprinkling motion two more times, first on the fire, then on me, redipping the red cloth each time.

"You and your mother shall be blessed," she said.

"God will protect you from all evil men. From vicious animals, bad spirits, and especially"—this last part she drew out dramatically—"from Jews."

Inwardly I gasped, but outwardly my reaction was little more than a slight widening of my eyes. My appreciation for a good joke nearly got the better of me as I fought off the giggles.

"Oh, thank you," I said, stifling the insane laughter welling inside of me.

"Let me pay you for your trouble." I reached for my little bundle and undid the kerchief. This called for a feat of bluffing and acting that would top even the performance given by my hostess. I revealed the two round stones.

"Oh, no!" I cried. "Oh, no! Look what my little brother has done! That bad boy has exchanged my eggs for these stones." I looked at her in horror.

"After the great good you have done me, to not be able to pay you properly. . . . He will get a beating for this, I will see to that!"

The old woman smiled benevolently. "Little brothers can be demons," she said.

"Come back tomorrow with the eggs, or a little flour, perhaps."

"Oh, thank you so much," I said. I was about to start feeling sorry for her and ashamed for what I had done, when I remembered how she had classified the Jewish people with vicious animals and bad spirits. I picked up my kerchief from the chair, mumbled something, walked to the door, and quickly closed it behind me.

I was afraid to meet the Ukrainian policemen again, so I hid in a wooden shack behind the Wrozka's hut until it was dark, and then found my way back to Wujciu's.

*

My Mother's Search

The man, who spoke in Yiddish, introduced himself as a representative of a British Immigrant Aid Society, a wholly charitable organization, whose purpose was to offer aid and comfort to friendless Jews arriving from foreign ports. He showed no surprise at our situation. He told us that we were the victims of unscrupulous travel agents in Russia who had sold us tickets to London while charging us for passage to New York. Ours was not an unusual case, and his society was prepared to look after us temporarily until it could locate our friends or relatives or fellow townsmen now residing in London. He then left us for a while and soon returned with a man trundling a pushcart. Our belongings were loaded on the cart and, led by the Samaritan, we left the wharf. (It was Tilbury Dock, I learned later.) After walking through miles of ghostly streets, we reached the dwelling that had been prepared for us or for unfortunates like us.

Before the man from the society left us, he explained the British monetary system to my mother and then put ten shillings in her hand. This sum, he assured her, would take care of us for a week in a section of London where food could be bought cheaply on the streets,

From *A Lost Paradise: Early Reminiscences* by Samuel Chotzinoff. Rept. 1975 (orig. 1953) © 1955 Reprinted with permission of Ayer Publishing Co., Salem, N.H.

practically at one's doorstep. Indeed, our dead-end street, as well as the entire district around it, proved to be one great outdoor market.

Our accommodations were two rooms in a two-story, dingy old house in a dead-end street off Commercial Road. Some rickety chairs, a table, two iron cots, and a small kerosene stove were all the furnishings. My mother, after disposing our belongings to the best practical advantage around our apartment, went out shopping. She returned with bread, herring, sugar, tea, and cottage cheese, and with grave doubts about the integrity of our benefactor, whose optimistic evaluation of the cost of living in London's ghetto she had discovered to be misleading. Things were, in fact, twice as dear as they were at *home*. From there on, to the end of their lives, Vitebsk remained "home" to my parents.

Notwithstanding the heartening, though limited, generosity of the society, our situation was decidedly depressing. That night, when I was supposed to be asleep, I heard my father and mother talking long and earnestly about our future. My father had little to suggest that was constructive. He spoke a good deal about "home," contrasting its remembered joys with the bleak, hopeless prospect now facing us. But my mother, as usual, put her whole mind to a consideration of ways and means for ameliorating our lot. "We can't just sit here, talking of home and waiting for something to happen," she said. "We must do *something*. Do we know anyone in London?" The query was obviously rhetorical, for my father did not deign to answer. "Don't tell me *nobody*," she cried. "There must be *somebody*. They say London is the largest city in the world, much bigger than New York. I don't know how many thousands live in London. So there must be somebody here from Vitebsk. . . . Think hard—Maybe you'll remember. . . There must have been somebody who went—*not* to America!"

There was a long silence and then my father said hesitatingly: "I seem to remember—I'm not sure—Aunt Rivka's son-in-law's brother. But you wouldn't know him. He left Ula and went to live in Vitebsk. It was years before we were married. Yes, now I recall—he left Vitebsk about twenty-five years ago."

My mother's voice sounded tense as she interrupted him: "Did he go to London?" My father was not sure. "Well, did he go to America?" my mother persisted. On that point my father was certain. He distinctly remembered that America was definitely the place the man had not gone to. "Well then," my mother cried triumphantly, "if he did not go to America, where else *could* he have gone to?"

My father ventured a suggestion: "Africa, maybe?" the absurdity of which my mother implied in her challenge: "And what would he be doing in Africa?" (Africa symbolized for my mother the extreme of strangeness or remoteness. "Africa," she would say by way of putting the finishing touch to a picture of faraway desolation, "where pepper grows!" For many years, I believed that the spice could flourish only in some desolate area of the dark continent.)

"Well," my mother went on, "there can be no doubt about it, Rivka's cousin, or whatever he was, *must* have gone to London. The question is how to find him. What was his name?"

My father gave this some thought, for it was a long time before he answered. "I think it was—was it?—yes, of course. Now it comes back to me. Horowitz, that's it—his name was Horowitz!"

My mother greeted this information with the elation of one who, after frantic cogitation, remembers a magic password. "Well," she said, "now we must *find* Horowitz. Didn't he have a first name?"

My father couldn't remember the first name, but wished to know how she proposed to locate Mr. Horowitz in a city the size of London. My mother could not say at the moment, but she thought the man from the society would help find him.

Within a few days he came to see how we were getting along, and she told him the little she knew about Mr. Horowitz. He said that he would do what he could. Several days later he reported to her that none of the Horowitzes he had been able to locate was the one she wanted. That evening I again overheard her and Father engaging in deep discussion.

"Let's see," she began. "Mr. Horowitz left Vitebsk about twenty-five years ago, you say. How old could he have been then?"

My father hazarded twenty-three or twenty-five. "That would make him now—let's see," and my mother made a rapid calculation, "about forty-eight or fifty, wouldn't it? What did he look like? But of course he'd be quite changed after all these years. Was he heavy-like? Thin? What color hair? Eyes?"

My father's information on all these points was inconclusive, but that didn't faze my mother.

"It doesn't matter," she declared, "and anyway it can't be helped. Now let's see—what did Mr. Horowitz do in Vitebsk?"

Mr. Horowitz had worked at odd jobs in Vitebsk. No clue there.

"Did he have any money?" It appeared he couldn't have had.

"Well then," my mother said, "since he had no money when he came here, he must have been obliged to go to work!"

At this point my father advanced the dreadful possibility that, for all he knew, the man might be dead. This my mother brushed aside as irrelevant to the execution of the plan she had by now formulated in her mind.

"Now, as a Jew, Horowitz would naturally live and work among Jews, wouldn't he?" My father agreed, and my mother pushed on to the heart of her plan. "People go to work in the early morning and they return home in the evening, don't they? Now, if Mr. Horowitz is alive—of *course* he's alive, a man of fifty—and if he is working—you agree that he *is* working—then he will be going to work at seven o'clock tomorrow morning somewhere in this very part of London, and at seven at night he will be returning to his home somewhere around here!"

I could hear her rise and walk across the room with decision, as if she had definitely disposed of the vexing question of our future in London.

"And now let's get some sleep," she said.

My mother spent the next day exploring the Whitechapel district, asking questions of storekeepers and pedestrians, watching the flow of traffic in the larger thoroughfares, and noting when and where it was heaviest. That night she discussed her strategy with my father, or rather she apprised him of it, and on the following morning at seven they took up positions on each side of Commercial Road at its junction with Leman Street.

"Watch out for men who look about fifty—a little younger or a little older," my mother told my father as they separated to take up their posts.

I accompanied them for a lark, for the discovery of Mr. Horowitz seemed a very remote possibility even to an imaginative child of six. When, an hour later, the stream of pedestrians had thinned out to a trickle, and my father, relinquishing his post, crossed over to join my mother for their return home, I felt that the quixotic adventure definitely had been proved a failure. My father had accosted only one likely prospect, and my mother had seen none who might conceivably be Mr. Horowitz. We walked home in silence, and I wondered what new scheme my mother would evolve now that Mr. Horowitz had proved nonexistent. But toward nightfall, as I played in our street with a new-found friend, I saw my parents leave the house and walk toward Whitechapel. I abandoned my playmate and joined them. At the corner of Commercial Road and Leman Street, they again took up their positions of the morning, and again for an hour scrutinized the hurrying passers-by, again without success.

Once my mother ran after a middle-aged man, caught him by his sleeve, and said: "Excuse me, you look so familiar. Did you ever live in Russia?"

The man, obviously astonished, stopped in his tracks, looked my mother over, and said: "Why, yes."

My mother then led him aside, away from the stream of fast-moving men and women. "Your name isn't—Horowitz?" The man shook his head and asked why. My mother made some hurried excuse, and he went on his way.

My father had accosted no one. At eight o'clock we again returned home. My mother busied herself with the evening meal while my father read his Talmud.

Days and weeks went by. Each Monday the man from the Aid Society appeared and placed ten shillings in my mother's hand. Our meals seemed never to vary. It was always herring, potatoes, bread, cheese, and tea. My father found himself a synagogue of the proper denomination, where he went three times a day, and my mother was endlessly engaged in shopping, cooking, scrubbing, and washing. But every morning and evening except Saturdays and Sundays they would both be at their posts in the London ghetto, patiently scanning the figures and faces of men hurrying by, occasionally stopping one and after a brief colloquy turning away to search for other possibilities. I soon lost all interest in the game and joined my parents only when I had nothing better to do.

A letter had been dispatched to our cousin in Passaic, apprising him of our recent misfortune and present predicament, and a reply came back expressing sympathy for our plight, but containing no constructive suggestions for its alleviation. In truth, there was nothing the man could do to help us, as it was unlikely that he possessed or would wish to part with a sum large enough to pay our passage to America. Furthermore, his kinship to us was not close enough to justify any great sacrifice on his part. There were certain things one could reasonably expect of a first cousin, but not of a second. The moral obligations of relatives were well defined among us, and people did only what they were expected to do. He did, however, urge us to "look around" and keep him posted. His offer of a temporary home in Passaic still stood.

As she grew more familiar with the neighborhood of her search, and to avoid being thought queer by the people in the shops, who were sure to wonder at her persistence, my mother shifted her operations to adjoining streets and avenues. She was "working" one of these side streets one evening. I had come along for the walk. The crowds had tapered off, and my father was signaling us from the opposite corner that it was time to go home. At the same moment a man in a gray bowler hat brushed past us. My mother looked at him and shot out a restraining hand. I had seen this happen many times during the past six weeks, and I tugged at her skirts, impatient to be off. But my mother's routine question had already stopped the man.

"Yes," he replied, "I come from Russia. Why do you ask?"

My mother disengaged her skirt from my grasp and went very close to the man. "Excuse me," she persisted, "perhaps from Vitebsk?"

The man regarded her wonderingly. "Why, yes," he said, "I come from Vitebsk."

This was, indeed, progress of a sort, and I began to share the excitement that I read in my mother's face.

Many men she had accosted had acknowledged Russia as their birth place, but none had even spoken the magic name of our native city. Still, any number of Vitebsk men might be living in London. Why should this man in the bowler hat be the one man we were seeking? Before I could wonder about him any further, my mother had breathlessly put to him her final question.

"Why, no," he answered quickly, "my name is Harris." He started on, but after a few steps he suddenly turned and came back to her. "As a matter of fact," he said slowly, "it *was* Horowitz. But that was a long time ago in Vitebsk. When I came to London, I changed it to Harris. Why do you ask?"

Without a word my mother clutched him to her heart. The man endured the embrace with equanimity, for my mother was then in her early thirties and quite handsome. My father, hoping that the miracle had finally occurred, now crossed the street on the run and, without seeking to know more, shoved my mother aside and in turn embraced Mr. Harris. I ran home alone to be the first to bear the good news to my brothers and sisters. A few minutes later my parents arrived with the now radiant Mr. Harris in tow. For Mr. Harris, on learning our identity and the nature and extent of the hunt that had been conducted for him, marveled at my mother's ingenuity and persistence, and expressed himself as very pleased to find himself so suddenly provided with a set of kinsfolk, "ready to wear, so to speak," he said.

❊

"Table Talk"

There lived in New York a formidable old lady named Mrs. Wolcott. Her life's business was lion hunting. She was an inveterate and almost invincible dinner-giver. So Big, Show Boat and The Royal Family had made me fair game for her. Thus far I had escaped her careful aim.

Then, one day, when I was off guard, she said that she was giving a dinner for eight. Winthrop Ames had said he would come if I would. I welcomed the thought of sitting next him at a small dinner and having an hour of his stimulating talk and his gay glancing wit.

There was good talk and good food. Winthrop sat between the hostess and me. The conversation turned to books, someone mentioned G. B. Stern's novel, The Matriarch, which had been well received.

"That book!" shouted the hostess. "When I found it was about spawning Jews I threw it across the room."

A little silence fell. It was, I suppose, just about the nastiest little silence I have ever felt. I said, with laborious dignity, "It was a rich chronicle of a dramatic and cultured family. I loved it."

In leaped the gallant Winthrop. "Dramatic! That's it!

—— 134 ——

I've often thought that if it hadn't been for the Jew in me I'd never have amounted to anything in the theater."

"*You*, Winthrop!" screeched Mrs. Wolcott.

"Certainly," he went on, equably. "Old Ameus, from whom we get our name of Ames. It's all in the book of the family tree in the library up at North Easton. Old Ameus, the Jew, who was thrown out of England and into Spain, and out of Spain back into England, centuries ago. Where do you suppose I get this profile, if not from him!"

"That," I put in, lamely, "is exactly the way I feel about it. We Jews, because we've been suppressed for centuries express ourselves in the creative arts and sciences."

"Oh, are you Jewish—too?" faltered our charming hostess. "I didn't know—"

"Only," I replied cheerfully, "on my mother's and father's side, my grandmothers' and grandfathers', my great-grandmothers' and great-grandfathers', my great-great-grand—"

"There are Jews and Jews," interrupted Mrs. W., graciously.

"Yes, indeed. And Christians *and* Christians." With which I took my departure.

※

III. Bibliography

A. BACKGROUND AND FOLKLORE

Baum, Hyman and Michel. *The Jewish Woman in America*. NY: Dial Press, 1976.

Brayer, Menachem. *The Jewish Woman in Rabbinic Literature*. Hoboken, NJ: KTAV, 1986.

Camp, Claudia. *Wisdom and the Feminine in the Book of Proverbs*. Decatur, Ga.: Almond Press, 1985.

Camp, Claudia, V. "The Wise Women of 2 Samuel: A Role Model for Women in Early Israel," *Catholic Biblical Quarterly*, 43: 14–29.

Cantor, Aviva, ed., *The Jewish Woman: 1900–85 Bibliography*. NY: Biblio Press, 1987. (See Jewish Women Non-Fiction USA and Canada for citations of biographies and women's memoirs)

Davidowicz, Lucy. *The Golden Tradition: Jewish Life and Thought in Eastern Europe*. Boston: Beacon, 1967.

Fink, Greta. *Great Jewish Women: Profiles of Courageous Women from the Maccabean Period to the Present*. NY: Menorah, 1978.

Haas, Peter J., ed. *Recovering the Role of Women: Power and Authority in Rabbinic Jewish Society*. Atlanta, Ga.: Scholars Press, 1992.

Koltuv, Barbara B. *The Book of Lilith*. York Beach, Me.: Nicolas-Hays, 1986.

M. Herschel Levine. "Three Talmudic Tales of Seduction," *Judaism*, Fall, 1987. pp.466–470.

Niditch, S., "Legends of Wise Heroes and Heroines," in *The Hebrew Bible and Its Modern Interpreters*, by D. A. Knight and G. M. Tucker. Philadelphia: Fortress Press, 1985.

Noy, Dov. *Studies in Jewish Folklore*. Hoboken, NJ: KTAV, 1981.

Ozick, Cynthia, "Notes Toward Finding the Right Question," in *On Being a Jewish Feminist, A Reader*. Ed., Susannah Heschel, Schocken Books, 1983.

Pardes, Ilana. *Counter-Traditions in the Bible: A Feminist Approach*. Belknap Press of Harvard. 1992.

Schram, Peninnah. *The Joys of Jewish Storytelling*, Jewish Book World, published by the Jewish Book Council, NY, Summer, 1990, v. 8, no. 3. (contains extensive bibliography) Note: This folklorist is continuing the tradition of master storytellers at the NY 92nd St. YM-YWHA, with yearly programs that include many women. In the early 20th century in East European towns there were Jewish "wise women" storytellers.

Schwarzbaum, Haim. *Studies in Jewish and World Folklore.* Hawthorne, NY: De Gruyter, 1968.

Schwarzbaum, Haim. *Jewish Folklore: An Annotated Bibliography.* NY & London, 1986.

Taitz, Emily and Henry, Sondra. *Written Out of History: Our Jewish Foremothers.* 2nd ed., 1990. NY: Biblio Press.

Unterman, Alan. *Dictionary of Jewish Lore and Legend.* NY: Thames & Hudson, 1991.

Wiesel, Elie. "Rabbi Meir and Brurya," in *Sages and Dreamers.* NY: Summit Books/Simon & Schuster, 1991.

Zuckoff, Aviva Cantor. "The Lilith Question," *Lilith* Mag., v.1,#1, Fall, 1976.

B. SELECTED MEMOIRS OF JEWISH WOMEN*

Antin, Mary. *The Promised Land.* Boston & NY: Houghton Mifflin Co. 1912 Reprinted 1969.

Chagall, Bella. *Burning Lights.* NY: Schocken, 1946.

Dash, Joan. *Summoned to Jerusalem: The Life of Henrietta Szold.* NY: Harper & Row, 1979.

Dryfoos, Susan W. *Iphigene: Memoirs of Iphigene Ochs Sulzberger of the New York Times family.* NY: Dodd, Mead, 1981.

Hillesum, Etty. *An Interrupted Life.* NY: Pantheon, 1983.

Hobson, Laura Z. *A Life.* NY: Arbor House, 1983.

LaZebnik, Edith. *Such A Life.* NY: William Morrow, 1978.

Leitner, Isabella. *Fragments of Isabella: A Memoir.* NY: Crowell, 1978.

Levy, Harriet Lane. *920 O'Farrell St.* Doubleday, 1947. Reprinted 1975 Arno.

Lixl-Purcell, Andreas, Ed. *Women of Exile: German-Jewish Autobiographies Since 1933.* Westport, Ct.: Greenwood Press, 1988.

Marcus, Jacob Rader. *Memoirs of American Jews, 1775–1865.* Philadelphia: Jewish Publication Society, 1955.

Meyer, Annie Nathan. *It's Been Fun.* NY: Henry Shuman, 1951.

Morton, Leah. (Pseud. Elizabeth G. Stern) *My Mother and I.* NY: Macmillan, 1917.

Pesotta, Rose. *Bread Upon The Waters.* NY: Dodd Mead, 1944.

Picon Molly. *Molly! An Autobiography.* NY: Simon & Schuster, 1980.

Schneiderman, Rose and Goldthwaite, Lucy. *All for One.* NY: Paul S. Erickson, 1967.

Shazar, Rachel Katznelson, Ed. *The Plough Woman: Memoirs of the Pioneer Women of Palestine.* NY: Herzl Press, 1975.

---

*For additional memoir sources, see excerpt permission credits in the text; also in *Memoir Authors* section following.

Sheklow, Edna. *So Talently My Children*. Cleveland: World, 1966.

Simon, Kate. *Bronx Primitive: Portraits In A Childhood*. NY: Viking, 1982.

Solomon, Hannah G. *Fabric of My Life: Autobiography of A Social Pioneer*. NY: Bloch Publishing Co., 1946.

Weinberg, Sydney Stahl. *The World Of Our Mothers. Lives Of Jewish Immigrant Women*. Chapel Hill: Univ. of N.C., 1989.

Winkler, Gershon; Greenspan, Marlene and Goldman, Reva S. *They Called Her Rebbe: The Maiden of Ludomir*. NY: Judaica Press, 1991.

Yezierska, Anzia. *Red Ribbon On A White Horse*, Rev. ed., NY: Persea Books, 1988.

Zipser, Arthur and Zipser, Pearl. *Fire and Grace: The Life of Rose Pastor Stokes*. Univ. of Georgia: 1990.

Zunser, Miriam Shomer. *Yesterday*. Harrisburg, Pa: Stackpole Sons, 1939.

IV. Memoir Authors

ALICIA APPLEMAN-JURMAN
   b. Buczacz, Poland; a Holocaust survivor who immigrated to the USA in 1952. She is the mother of three grown children and lives in California with her husband. Her book, *Alicia: My Story* received the 1989 Christopher Award.

GERTRUDE BERG 1899–1966
   b. Gertrude Edelstein, NY, author, producer and actress of "The Rise of the Goldbergs," a famous radio series, later TV, of a Jewish family, based on her family milieu. During 30's and 40's she wrote screenplays and hundreds of scripts; and during 1959–62, played the lead in a Broadway show, A Majority Of One. Earlier she performed in vaudeville with sketches of a Catskill mountain resort owned by her father, which was published as *House of Glass*. In 1961 she published her memoir, *Molly and Me*.

RACHEL CALOF 1876–1952
   b. Rachel Bella Kahn in the Ukraine, orphaned at an early age, she left Russia via an arranged marriage to Abraham Calof, who had already emigrated to the US. She arrived in 1894, moving to a homestead 20 miles from Devil's Lake, N.D. The Calofs lived there for 23 years where she had five daughters and four sons. She later moved to Seattle where she died at 76.

KIM CHERNIN 1940–
   b. NY; now a Californian, a "feminist humanist" writer and editor. *In My Mother's House* from which our excerpt derives, she has called "fictional biography." Other books are: *The Obsession: Reflections on the Tyranny of Slenderness, The Hungry Self, Reinventing Eve*, and forthcoming, *Crossing the Border: An Erotic Journey*.

SAMUEL C. CHOTZINOFF 1889–1964
   Pianist, writer, music critic for the New York Post during the 1930's. He was music consultant to National Broadcasting Co., later producing NBC/TV operas. His one book from which our excerpt is taken is *A Lost Paradise: Early Reminiscences*, originally published 1953.

EDNA FERBER 1887–1968
   b. Kalamazoo; novelist, short story writer, journalist and playwright. Her work spans four decades, with a Pulitzer received in 1924 for *So Big*. She

was first a reporter in Appleton, WI; then in Milwaukee, and during W.W. 2 was a war correspondent. Her well-known novels were filmed (Giant, Show Boat, Dinner At Eight, etc.) Her last popular novel in 1960 was *Ice Palace*. Her plays are still performed: *Stage Door, The Royal Family, Show Boat*. In the 20's and 30's she was called "the greatest" among American women novelists. Her autobiography, *A Peculiar Treasure*, dwells in detail on her Jewishness.

GLUCKEL OF HAMELN 1645–1724

A Yiddish memoirist from a prominent family of Hamburg, Germany. Married at 14, she had 12 children. After her husband's death, she continued his business and remarried to Cerf Levy of Metz, she began her memoirs at 46, paused for 16 years and resumed in 1719. They were published in 1896 and became a source for information about Jewish history and culture of the towns of 17th century Berlin. A biography of her life is by B. Z. Abrahams, *Life of Glueckel of Hameln*, 1962.

EMMA GOLDMAN 1859–1940

b. Kovno, Lithuania; emigrated to USA 1885. She became a leading anarchist and writer, via her journal, "Mother Earth" during 1906–18. Opposing W.W. 1 conscription, she went to jail and was deported to the Soviet Union in 1919, but left there 1921, disillusioned with the lack of equal rights after the revolution. She lived in many countries of Europe thereafter, and Canada. In addition to her own autobiography, Richard Drinnon has written *Rebel in Paradise*, 1961. Her *Letters from Exile*, Chap. 3, by Drinnon, sheds more light on our excerpt.

MARIE JASTROW 1897–1991

b. Marie Grunfeld in Danzig (now Gdansk, Poland); lived in Yugoslavia, then immigrated to US in 1907 and settled in NYC; later moving to Tucson, AZ. She devoted her mature years to her family, writing her first book at age 82, 1979 from which our excerpt is derived, and the second, *Looking Back: The American Dream Through Immigrant Eyes, 1907–1918*, published in 1986. Her son, Robert Jastrow, the astrophysicist, directs the Mount Wilson Institute in Pasadena, CA.

REBECCA KOHUT 1864–1951

b. Kaschau, Slovakia; emigrated to the US as a child. She was known as an educator, vocational guide and Jewish community leader, founding the Kohut School for Girls. In 1914 she led the YMHA's Employment Bureau, and in 1931 was appointed to the NY State Employment Commission. She is remembered for her work as president of the World Council of Jewish Women in 1942 and thereafter. Her autobiography in 1925 was *My Portion;* and *More Yesterdays*, in 1950. She wrote about her husband, George Alexander Kohut, in 1936.

GOLDA MEIR 1898–1978

b. Golda Mabovitch in Kiev, Russia; came to the US in 1906 with her family to Milwaukee. Emigrated to Palestine 1921 after her sister. She had a notable career there in the 20's and 30's, rising to the leadership of the Histadrut. She became Minister of Labor in the first Knesset of statehood in 1949. In 1956 she became Foreign Minister until 1965, and a prime spokesperson for Israel's interests. In 1969 she became the fourth Prime Minister of Israel.

FAYE MOSKOWITZ, n.d.

An essayist and journalist who has written for the *Washington Post* and the *New York Times* Hers column. She lives in Washington, DC with her husband and four grown children, where she is a director and teacher at the Edmund Burke School. Her other books are: *And The Bridge Is Love: Life Stories* (1991), and *Whoever Finds This, I Love You* (1992).

ERNESTINE L. ROSE 1810–1892

b. Ernestine Louise Potowski in Piotrkow, Poland, daughter of a rabbi. At 17 she left for Germany; then France and England, where she married William Rose, a follower of the utopian socialist Robert Owen. They came to America in 1836 and remained until 1874. From 1836–70, Rose was an active suffragist and reformer for women's rights, and in demand as a speaker, associated with Elizabeth Cady Stanton. The only biography of her life is by Yuri Suhl, cited in our excerpt.

SOPHIE RUSKAY 1885–1980

b. NYC to a Russian family of seven, in which she was the only female. Attended Barnard College, and there began a lifelong career of service to Jewish communal causes, serving on the national boards of Hadassah, The Women's League, and the NYC Federation of Jewish Philanthropies, among others. She published three books in addition to *Horsecars and Cobblestones: Discovery at Aspen* and *The Jelly Women*.

ISAAC BASHEVIS SINGER 1904–1991

b. Radzymin, Poland, son of a Hassidic rabbi. Came to US in 1935, and in New York City became a prolific author of Yiddish fiction and essays for Yiddish newspapers, depicting life in East European shtetls. He had many translators and awards, including the National Book Award, crowned with the Nobel prize for literature in 1978. His best known novels are *Gimpel the Fool, The Slave,* and *Zlateh the Goat* (for juveniles). Two films were made of his fiction, *Enemies, A Love Story,* and *Yentl, The Yeshiva Boy.*

ELIZABETH GERTRUDE STERN 1890–1954

An American social worker who made her way into journalism and management. She wrote under her own name, Leah Morton, and her pseudonym: *When Love Comes to Woman; My Mother and I, This Ecstasy, A Friend At Court, Women Behind Gandhi,* in addition to her best known work, *I Am A Woman And A Jew,* from which our excerpt derives.

LISELOTTE BENDIX STERN 1918–

b. Berlin, Germany, to parents who later perished in the Holocaust. Emigrated to England in 1939 and to the USA in 1940. Worked in various occupations: nursing, governess, cook, lab technician, medical indexer and behavioral sciences librarian. Married Max M. Stern, M.D., psychoanalyst, later assisting with publication of his posthumous work, *Repetition and Trauma,* 1988. Currently a volunteer advocate on homelessness and housing.

HANNAH TRAGER 1870–1943

b. England and brought to Palestine when 2 years old. Her father moved the family 15 times from London to Palestine between 1871–1906. She was educated in London, married and raised a family, returning to Palestine in the late 1920's. She wrote three books in English, reflecting a youthful point of view about growing up in a settlement in Palestine.

SOPHIE TRUPIN n.d.

See book from which our excerpt derives, Dakota Diaspora, for information. (A recent video shown on public television, included Sophie Trupin and her husband, in a series, P.O.V., Point of View)